MALACHI

and the great and dreadful day

Mark E. Petersen

Deseret Book Company
Salt Lake City, Utah

Printed in the United States of America
ISBN 0-87747-962-3

First printing March 1983

CONTENTS

1	Prophecies for Today	1
2	Who Was Malachi?	4
3	Blemished Sacrifices	7
4	Will a Man Rob God?	11
5	The Savior and Malachi	15
6	Joseph the Forerunner	19
7	Joseph the Temple Builder	22
8	The Wilderness Tabernacle	25
9	Subsequent Temples	29
10	The Predicted Judgment	32
11	The Preparation	37
12	Elijah the Prophet	39
13	Elijah Translated	42
14	Elijah's Mission	46
15	The Sealing Keys	49
16	To Redeem the Dead	53
17	Elijah's Visitation	56
18	Research Follows	58
19	Salvation for Living and Dead	63
20	What of Baptism?	68
21	The Hearts Did Turn	72
	Index	75

Chapter 1

PROPHECIES FOR TODAY

Out of the past, Malachi speaks vigorously to our present generation. His messages, though brief, have a direct relationship to our day. Partially fulfilled in the restoration of the gospel through the Prophet Joseph Smith, they also point to events yet future, even to the opening of the Millennium.

The Savior considered Malachi's prophecies as being so important that he quoted some of them to the Nephites, who had never heard of them before. While Jesus was with those ancient Americans, he told them that the writings of Malachi were so vital that the Father himself had commanded that they should be given to them. (See 3 Nephi 24:1.)

Malachi lived nearly two hundred years after Lehi left Jerusalem; hence that prophet had no access to his writings. But the Lord provided them, explaining: "These scriptures, which ye had not with you, the Father commanded that I should give unto you; for it was wisdom in him that they should be given unto future generations." (3 Nephi 26:2.)

Why to future generations? Because those were the peoples who would see their fulfillment. Malachi's writings would be a voice of warning and a guiding light to them.

To certify that Malachi's prophecies refer to the latter days, the Nephite scriptures go on to say that Jesus "did expound all things, even from the beginning until the time that he should come in his glory—yea, even all things which should come upon the face of the earth, even until the elements should melt with fervent heat, and the earth should be wrapt together as a scroll, and the heavens and the earth should pass away;

"And even unto the great and last day, when all people, and all kindreds, and all nations and tongues shall stand before God, to be judged of their works, whether they be good or whether they be evil—

"If they be good, to the resurrection of everlasting life; and if they be evil, to the resurrection of damnation; being on a parallel, the one on the one hand and the other on the other hand, according to the mercy, and the justice, and the holiness which is in Christ, who was before the world began." (3 Nephi 26:3-5.)

It is most significant that the Father himself gave Malachi the revelations that form that prophet's prophecies relating so directly to the time in which we live. The Savior made this known as he quoted Malachi to the Nephites. "Thus said the Father unto Malachi," he declared. (3 Nephi 24:1.)

Like Isaiah, Malachi addressed the people of his own day about their particular problems, but also like Isaiah, he foretold some of the greatest events of latter days.

He provided further details concerning the Second Coming of Christ and the spectacular, world-shaking nature of that event.

He declared that a special messenger would prepare the way for the Lord's great appearance. That messenger was the prophet Joseph Smith.

He predicted that when the Lord appears, he will "suddenly come to his temple," thus affirming that the Saints of latter days would be a temple-building people. Otherwise, how could the Lord come to a temple designated as his own?

To dispel any doubt about this glorious coming, the prophet further emphasized: "Behold he shall come, saith the Lord of hosts." (Malachi 3:1.)

He described that time as a period of great tribulation, and asked, "Who may abide the day of his coming?" (Malachi 3:2.)

Malachi predicted one of the most significant events of the entire latter-day period, the return to earth of the Prophet Elijah, who would turn the hearts of the fathers and the children toward each other. This visitation was to open the doors for the genealogical and temple program of the Saints; without it, the earth would be smitten with a curse. But Elijah came, and the curse was stayed. Then was not Malachi a prophet for our time, even as was Isaiah?

Another aspect to his mission had deep meaning. He lived in a day of apostasy. Many Jews had rejected their God, embraced pagan deities, and married heathen wives.

We, too, live in a day of apostasy when the Christ is being rejected by millions. He seeks to gather the nations, and especially his covenant people, as a hen gathers her chickens under her wings. But relatively few come.

The means by which Malachi tried to persuade the ancient Jews to serve the Lord are little different from our persuasions of today, as wayward modern peoples turn to other interests.

Yes, Malachi's writings are important to us here and now. When the Savior said that the prophet's message was to be for future generations, he was speaking of us.

Chapter 2

WHO WAS MALACHI?

Historically, little is recorded about Malachi, but modern revelation provides additional information.

The name Malachi means literally "my messenger." It thus signifies "the messenger of Jehovah" or the "angel of Jehovah." No details of his personal life have been preserved. It is known that he ministered about 440 B.C. and that he was contemporary with the period of Nehemiah. He lived at the time of the Jews' return from their Babylonian captivity and saw the reconstruction of the temple in Jerusalem.

The Jews of that time had not yet learned the lesson intended through their captivity, for many still turned to idolatry, which had contaminated them in Babylon. Even some of the priests married heathen women, divorcing their lawful wives to do so. The great thrust of the ministries of that day was to maintain the worship of Jehovah in the face of the growing apostasy.

During the seventy years of their Babylonian captivity, the Jews were sifted throughout the empire. They were not kept together at one site. Many of them intermarried with the local population and thus spread from one end of the nation to the other. This was further fulfillment of the prediction that they would be scattered among the nations.

It is not known how many Jews actually were carried away into Babylon, but it is well accepted that only a portion of them returned to Jerusalem when Cyrus the Great opened the door for this event.

As is seen from the books of Daniel, Ezra, Nehemiah, and others, tremendous pressure was exerted upon the Jews to turn from their traditional religion and accept the idolatry of their captors. The story of Nebuchadnezzar and the fiery furnace is a well-known example. (See Daniel 3.)

Ezra had lived for a time in Babylon, where he grieved over the wickedness of the chosen people. He cried out at one time, "O my God, I am ashamed and blush to lift up my face to thee, my God: for our iniquities are increased over our head, and our trespass is grown up unto the heavens." (Ezra 9:6.)

Ezra came to Jerusalem about 458 B.C. Nehemiah arrived thirteen years later, in 445, and the two men worked together for the reformation of their people. Then came Malachi, who joined them in this effort. His writings are believed to date between 445 and 432 B.C.

Many of the Jewish priests apostatized and introduced idolatrous practices, corrupting the true worship of the living God. Scholars say that their rituals were "empty, worthless and perfunctory," void of all spiritual power. According to the *New Analytical Bible and Dictionary of the Bible,* "The great task of Ezra, Nehemiah and Malachi was to bring the people to a profound consciousness of their covenant obligations, to deepen their spiritual life, to arouse the spirit of true worship and render an acceptable service to God." (Chicago: John A. Dickson Publishing Co., c.1941.)

Malachi rebuked the wayward priests and their followers with great vigor, seeking to turn their minds back to the true God, but the success of these efforts, as well as those of Ezra and Nehemiah, was marginal at best. Not long afterward rebellious sects of various kinds were formed among the Jews, leading in turn to the persecutions and ultimate crucifixion of the Savior a few centuries later. At least a half dozen of these sects broke away from the traditional teachings and practices of the Mosaic law in this period. They were denounced fiercely by the Savior in his day.

In our modern scriptures, references to Malachi are not limited to the Book of Mormon passages provided by the Savior. They are also found in the Doctrine and Covenants, particularly concerning the coming of Elijah. There we read of the appearance of Elijah in the Kirtland Temple, where he himself spoke of Malachi and said, "Behold, the time has fully come, which was spoken of by the mouth of Malachi—testifying that he [Elijah] should be sent, before the great and dreadful day of the Lord." (D&C 110:14.)

Malachi's description of the day that shall "burn as an oven" is mentioned in Doctrine & Covenants 133:64. When Moroni came for the first time to Joseph Smith, he quoted Malachi, referring both to the day of vengeance and to the visitation of Elijah, again predicting his coming lest "the whole earth would be utterly wasted" at the appearance of the Lord. (Joseph Smith—History 1:39.)

President Joseph F. Smith, in his vision of the spirit world, referred to various personages he saw there, and among them was Malachi. (D&C 138:46.)

These passages should be regarded as confirmation of the actuality of the life and labors of Malachi, that he was indeed a prophet of God as indicated in the Bible, and also that his messages were true and had modern significance. The predictions he made relate clearly to this dispensation. Some have been fulfilled; others await the future.

Malachi was a reality. He was an inspired prophet and was accepted fully by God and angels, since he was quoted by both.

Chapter 3

BLEMISHED SACRIFICES

At no time has the Lord been willing to accept an unworthy sacrifice. This was true in the days of Cain and Abel; it was true in the time of Moses; and it is true in our own day. Malachi likewise denounced blemished sacrifices in his day.

When Moses gave the law that the priests of Malachi's day professed to follow, he made it abundantly clear that there must be no blemish on or in anything offered to the Lord. He said:

"Ye shall offer at your own will a male without blemish, of the beeves, of the sheep, or of the goats. But whatsoever hath a blemish, that shall ye not offer: for it shall not be acceptable for you.

"And whosoever offereth a sacrifice of peace offerings unto the Lord to accomplish his vow, or a freewill offering in beeves or sheep, it shall be perfect to be accepted; there shall be no blemish therein.

"Blind, or broken, or maimed, or having a wen, or scurvy, or scabbed, ye shall not offer these unto the Lord, nor make an offering by fire of them upon the altar unto the Lord. . . . Ye shall not offer unto the Lord that which is bruised, or crushed, or broken, or cut; neither shall ye make any offering thereof in your land." (Leviticus 22:19-22, 24.)

The law was carried a step further when Moses declared: "All the firstling males that come of thy herd and of thy flock thou shalt sanctify unto the Lord thy God: Thou shalt do no work with the firstling of thy bullock, nor shear the firstling of thy sheep. . . . And if there be any blemish therein, as if it be lame, or blind, or have any ill blemish, thou shalt not sacrifice it unto the Lord thy God." (Deuteronomy 15:19, 21.)

It is interesting that the Lord even prohibited the Jews from working an animal before it was sacrificed; neither could they shear a sheep intended for that purpose. The offering must be whole, with no deductions.

But in Malachi's day the priests disregarded the divine law, and for this wickedness the prophet upbraided them. One can almost hear his ringing tones as he said: "And if ye offer the blind for sacrifice, is it not evil? and if ye offer the lame and sick, is it not evil? offer it now unto thy governor; will he be pleased with thee, or accept thy person? saith the Lord of hosts." (Malachi 1:8.)

If it would not please the governor, how could the priests expect the Lord to accept it? So he declared: "Cursed be the deceiver, which hath in his flock a male, and voweth, and sacrificeth unto the Lord a corrupt thing: for I am a great King, saith the Lord of hosts, and my name is dreadful among the heathen." (Malachi 1:14.)

In righteous indignation the Lord spoke further through his prophet: "And now, O ye priests, this commandment is for you. If ye will not hear, and if ye will not lay it to heart, to give glory unto my name, saith the Lord of hosts, I will even send a curse upon you, and I will curse your blessings: yea, I have cursed them already, because ye do not lay it to heart. Behold, I will corrupt your seed, and spread dung upon your faces, even the dung of your solemn feasts; and one shall take you away with it." (Malachi 2:1-3.)

It was not only in the matter of polluted sacrifices that the prophet was concerned. One of the great evils of the Jews of that day was rejection of their legal wives, women of their own race and religion, and their marriages to heathen women who worshipped false gods. Malachi declared:

"Judah hath dealt treacherously, and an abomination is committed in Israel and in Jerusalem; for Judah hath profaned the holiness of the Lord which he loved, and hath married the daughter of a strange god.

"The Lord will cut off the man that doeth this, the master and the scholar, out of the tabernacles of Jacob, and him that offereth an offering unto the Lord of hosts.

"And this have ye done again, covering the altar of the Lord with tears, with weeping, and with crying out, insomuch that he regardeth not the offering any more, or receiveth it with good will at your hand.

"Yet ye say, Wherefore? Because the Lord hath been witness between thee and the wife of thy youth, against whom thou hast dealt treacherously: yet is she thy companion, and the wife of thy covenant.

"And did not he make one? Yet had he the residue of the spirit. And wherefore one? That he might seek a godly seed. Therefore take heed to your spirit, and let none deal treacherously against the wife of his youth." (Malachi 2:11-15.)

There is great purpose in honorable marriage within one's own faith. The Jews were a covenant tribe of Israel. The Lord wished to preserve a pure line of believers in the families of that people and to avoid any infusion of heathen beliefs among them. He sought to preserve good Israelitish marriages, as Malachi said, in order "that he might seek a godly seed," a believing and obedient offspring. There was also a matter of honor to be considered, honor as between men and women. When any man dealt treacherously "with the wife of his youth," it was considered an abomination in the sight of God.

Malachi and his fellow prophets realized the importance of approved marriages and good families, and they preached earnestly against the evils of mixed relationships.

When Nehemiah addressed the same subject, he ruled against marital relationships with unbelievers and said: "Ye shall not give your daughters unto their sons, nor take their daughters unto your sons, or for yourselves."

He spoke of the downfall of Solomon through this same kind of transgression: "Did not Solomon king of Israel sin by these things? yet among many nations was there no king like him, who was beloved of his God, and God made him king over all Israel: nevertheless even him did outlandish women cause to sin. Shall we then hearken unto you to do all this great evil, to transgress against our God in marrying strange wives?" (Nehemiah 13:25-27.)

Moses had warned his people of this problem: "Neither shalt thou make marriages with them; thy daughter thou shalt not give unto his son, nor his daughter shalt thou take unto thy son. *For they will turn away thy son from following me, that they may serve other gods:* so will the anger of the Lord be kindled against you, and destroy thee suddenly." (Deuteronomy 7:3-4.)

Moses provides the answer. He gives the divine reasoning. Obedience to the Lord was the only means of salvation. To follow after false gods could mean apostasy and eventual destruction.

The Lord was very direct when he said: "Let them marry to whom they think best; only to the family of the tribe of their father shall they marry. . . . And every daughter, that possesseth an inheritance in any tribe of the children of Israel, shall be wife unto one of the family of the tribe of her father, that the children of Israel may enjoy every man the inheritance of his fathers." (Numbers 36:6, 8.)

It was from these laws that the priests of Malachi's day had departed, and as they did so, they led others into the same erroneous paths.

In our own day the divine word on obedience reads: "But he that doeth not anything until he is commanded, and receiveth a commandment with doubtful heart, and keepeth it with slothfulness, the same is damned." (D&C 58:29.)

Chapter 4

WILL A MAN ROB GOD?

There are various ways by which mankind may rob the Lord. Malachi dealt with one of them as he condemned the wicked priests for offering blemished sacrifices to the Lord. Now he approached them directly and sharply on the matter of the ancient law of the tithe. To withhold these tithes was comparable to offering burnt sacrifices with blemishes.

Malachi's approach to this subject is all the more impressive when it is realized that the Savior himself used the prophet's words in teaching tithing to the Nephites. (See 3 Nephi 24.)

Is this something we may casually ignore? Is any direct command of the Lord really optional?

Malachi asked: "Will a man rob God?"

This is a hard question, especially when we realize that all that we have on earth comes from Him. Ingratitude is indeed an offense to the Almighty; it is an offense to humans as well.

God is the great Provider, and he commands us to be thankful in all things. When he gave the Saints in our day a restatement of some of the Ten Commandments, he said:

"Thou shalt thank the Lord thy God in all things." (D&C 59:7.) This is the law on gratitude. In the Doctrine and Covenants it stands all alone, in a paragraph by itself, and is given equal emphasis with the other commandments:

"Thou shalt love the Lord thy God. . . .

"Thou shalt love thy neighbor as thyself. Thou shalt not steal; neither commit adultery, nor kill, nor do anything like unto it. . . .

"Thou shalt offer a sacrifice unto the Lord thy God in righteousness, even that of a broken heart and a contrite spirit.

". . . Thou shalt go to the house of prayer and offer up thy sacraments upon my holy day." (D&C 59:5-6, 8-9.)

Yes, these are some of his great laws, and one of them teaches gratitude.

Would anyone purposely rob his greatest Benefactor? That Benefactor is God! He gave us all things; he asks only for a tithe in return. To pay it is a sign of appreciation. To refuse indicates sheer thanklessness.

Is withholding from God, then, some degree of robbery?

Malachi said so. He said: "Will a man rob God? Yet ye have robbed me. But ye say, Wherein have we robbed thee? In tithes and offerings. Ye are cursed with a curse: for ye have robbed me, even this whole nation.

"Bring ye all the tithes into the storehouse, that there may be meat in mine house, and prove me now herewith, saith the Lord of hosts, if I will not open you the windows of heaven, and pour you out a blessing, that there shall not be room enough to receive it.

"And I will rebuke the devourer for your sakes, and he shall not destroy the fruits of your ground; neither shall your vine cast her fruit before the time in the field, saith the Lord of hosts. And all nations shall call you blessed: for ye shall be a delightsome land, saith the Lord of hosts." (Malachi 3:8-12.)

What a promise! What a great blessing is offered if we will but obey!

"Bring ye all the tithes into the storehouse." That is a command with a promise of peace and prosperity. Is it not desirable to have the Lord rebuke the devourer (our enemies) for our sakes? And what a promise of bounteous harvests! What a joy to live "in a delightsome land"!

Malachi reminded his people that "even from the days of your fathers ye are gone away from mine ordinances, and have not kept them. Return unto me, and I will return unto you, saith the Lord of hosts. But ye said, Wherein shall we return?" (Malachi 3:7.)

Let them not follow the example of their fathers! Let them not rob God! Let them obey! Then will the windows of heaven open, and blessings beyond their ability to contain will be forthcoming.

Will anyone say that he cannot afford to pay tithing, when these facts are presented fairly to him? It is a law of prosperity and of peace. Truly, sacrifice brings forth the blessings of heaven. Truly the Lord is mindful of his own. Truly he is a God who cannot lie!

Abraham paid tithes of all he possessed. (See Genesis 14:20.)

The prophet Alma, whose writings appear in the Book of Mormon, referred to Abraham and his payment of tithing: "Yea, humble yourselves even as the people in the days of Melchizedek, who was also a high priest after this same order which I have spoken, who also took upon him the high priesthood forever. And it was this same Melchizedek to whom Abraham paid tithes; yea, even our father Abraham paid tithes of one-tenth part of all he possessed." (Alma 13:14-15.)

Moses also taught tithing. He said: "And all the tithe of the land, whether of the seed of the land, or of the fruit of the tree, is the Lord's: it is holy unto the Lord. And if a man will at all redeem ought of his tithes, he shall add thereto the fifth part thereof. And concerning the tithe of the herd, or of the flock, even of whatsoever passeth under the rod, the tenth shall be holy unto the Lord." (Leviticus 27:30-32.)

In his address recorded in Deuteronomy, Moses reemphasized his instructions: "Thou shalt truly tithe all the increase of thy seed, that the field bringeth forth year by year. And thou shalt eat before the Lord thy God, in the place which he shall choose to place his name there, the tithe of thy corn, of thy wine, and of thine oil, and the firstlings of thy herds and of thy flocks; that thou mayest learn to fear the Lord thy God always." (Deuteronomy 14:22-23.)

And to the Latter-day Saints, through the Prophet Joseph Smith, God taught this same precept, explaining that it "shall be a standing law unto them forever." (D&C 119:4.) He concluded this instruction with these words: "And I say unto you, if my people observe not this law, to keep it holy, and by this law sanctify the land of Zion unto me, that my statutes and my judgments may be kept thereon, that it may be most holy, behold, verily I say unto you, it shall not be a land of Zion unto you. And this shall be an ensample unto all the stakes of Zion. Even so. Amen." (D&C 119:6-7.)

Then shall we not obey? Will a man rob God?

Chapter 5

THE SAVIOR AND MALACHI

When the Savior was on the earth in the Meridian of Time, he stressed the importance of studying the scriptures. He commanded that we search them because they testify of him. (John 5:39.)

It is important that as we learn of him, we take upon us his yoke, a burden that all followers of Christ should assume. (See Matthew 11:28-30.) In this way, we come unto him. He desires that we come into his Kingdom intelligently, and that, of course, requires that we learn all we can about him.

The plan of the Lord is that eventually all scriptures will be given to us. Even the sealed portion of the Book of Mormon will be revealed when the proper time comes. The Savior explained:

"For I command all men, both in the east and in the west, and in the north, and in the south, and in the islands of the sea, that they shall write the words which I speak unto them; for out of the books which shall be written I will judge the world, every man according to their works, according to that which is written.

"For behold, I shall speak unto the Jews and they shall write it; and I shall also speak unto the Nephites and they shall write it; and I shall also speak unto the other tribes of the house of Israel, which I have led away, and they shall write it; and I shall also speak unto all nations of the earth and they shall write it.

"And it shall come to pass that the Jews shall have the words of the Nephites, and the Nephites shall have the words of the Jews; and the Nephites and the Jews shall have the words of the lost tribes of Israel; and the lost tribes of Israel shall have the words of the Nephites and the Jews." (2 Nephi 29:11-13.)

He said that as he will gather his various tribes in one, so will he gather his scriptures in one. (2 Nephi 29:14.) And for what purpose? He explained: "For behold, out of the books which have been written, and which shall be written, shall this people be judged, for by them shall their works be known unto men." Have not the prophets taught for ages that "out of the books which shall be written shall the world be judged?" What books? The book of life, of course, wherein our deeds are recorded, but also the scriptures. (3 Nephi 27:25-26.)

It is through reading the scriptures that we learn what the Lord requires of us. If we do not know these requirements, how can we live them? There are two reasons why it is our responsibility to read the scriptures and know what the Lord's requirements are: that we may obey them and obtain our salvation, and that we may know by what rules we shall be judged at the last day.

In modern times, the Lord has again commanded us to study the scriptures, and not just the sacred writings, but all good books. He believes in education, for we know that the glory of God is intelligence and that no one can be saved in ignorance. (D&C 88:118; 109: 7-14; 131:6.)

So it was that the Savior desired to give to the Nephites the words of Malachi, which were part of the Jewish scriptures, but which came after Lehi left Jerusalem. Hence, he quoted Malachi to them. The Book of Mormon reads: "And it came to pass that he commanded them [the Nephites] that they should write the words which the Father had given unto Malachi, which he should tell unto them."

Jesus said: "Behold, I will send my messenger, and he shall prepare the way before me, and the Lord whom ye seek shall suddenly come to his temple, even the messenger of the covenant. . . .

"But who may abide the day of his coming, and who shall stand when he appeareth? For he is like a refiner's fire, and like fuller's soap. And he shall sit as a refiner and purifier of silver; and he shall purify the sons of Levi, and purge them as gold and silver, that they may offer unto the Lord an offering in righteousness.

"Then shall the offering of Judah and Jerusalem be pleasant unto the Lord, as in the days of old, and as in former years." (3 Nephi 24:1-4.)

The Savior continued to quote Malachi's words exactly as they appear in the King James Version of the Bible. He did not hesitate when he came to the passages on tithing. His words were direct, just as they appear in Malachi. (See 3 Nephi 24: 8-12.)

He continued on and discussed his second coming:

"For behold, the day cometh that shall burn as an oven; and all the proud, yea, and all that do wickedly, shall be stubble; and the day that cometh shall burn them up, saith the Lord of hosts, that it shall leave them neither root nor branch.

"But unto you that fear my name, shall the Son of Righteousness arise with healing in his wings; and ye shall go forth and grow up as calves in the stall." (3 Nephi 25:1-2.)

He moved from the Bible version at this point and went directly to the prophecy on the return of Elijah the prophet:

"Behold, I will send you Elijah the prophet before the coming of the great and dreadful day of the Lord;

"And he shall turn the heart of the fathers to the children, and the heart of the children to their fathers, lest I come and smite the earth with a curse." (3 Nephi 25:5-6.)

It is to be noted particularly that those portions of Malachi which referred to the people in Jerusalem at his time, rebuking them for their sins, were omitted by the Savior as he spoke to the Nephites. To them he stressed those portions of Malachi which referred more to future generations, even the time in which we live. These are the words that he commanded the Nephites to write, and these are the words that the Nephites wrote in obedience to his command. They now appear in chapters 24 and 25 of Third Nephi.

Malachi's words, as quoted by the Savior, parallel the King James Version verbatim. Is not this a mighty confirmation of the accuracy of that version of the Bible? The same is true of most of the Isaiah excerpts as they appear in the Book of Mormon, not to mention the remarkable Sermon on the Mount. The

Book of Mormon is a direct translation from gold plates, provided through Joseph Smith and the Urim and Thummim. Such inspiration allowed for no mistakes. The message is the same as God himself gave to Malachi, and it was confirmed by the Son of God as he quoted the words of his Father.

Some critics claim that Joseph Smith made the Bible inserts in the Book of Mormon on his own, by his own wisdom, seeking to make a better book.

This, of course, is ridiculous. Joseph was "an unlearned man," as Isaiah said (Isaiah 29:11-12), and in no way did he either write the Book of Mormon by himself or insert any of the excerpts from the Bible. The Book of Mormon was translated by the power of God and not of man. (See D&C, sections 5 and 10.)

Therefore, the Book of Mormon is indeed a witness to the accuracy of the King James Version of the Bible, which is the authorized text used by The Church of Jesus Christ of Latter-day Saints. And as Isaiah himself described the Book of Mormon, it is a marvelous work and a wonder.

Chapter 6

JOSEPH THE FORERUNNER

Who prepared the way for the Second Coming of the Lord Jesus Christ? Who prepared the way for his first coming?

As John the Baptist was the forerunner of the Lord's mortal advent, so the Prophet Joseph Smith was raised up as the forerunner, or messenger, to prepare for the glorious Second Coming of the Savior.

In Malachi we read: "Behold, I will send my messenger, and he shall prepare the way before me: and the Lord, whom ye seek, shall suddenly come to his temple, even the messenger of the covenant, whom ye delight in: behold, he shall come, saith the Lord of hosts." (Malachi 3:1.)

How did John prepare the way for the first coming of Jesus? By preaching the gospel, crying repentance to an apostate world, and heralding the One "mightier than I . . . the latchet of whose shoes I am not worthy to unloose." (Luke 3:16.)

John came preaching baptism for the remission of sins and said that Christ would baptize "with the Holy Ghost and with fire." In his preparation for the Savior, he was to preach the gospel so effectively that he would convert a body of believers to accept Jesus when he appeared. (Luke 1:17.)

A similar commission was given to Joseph Smith. He too was to prepare a people to receive the Lord. And how was this to be accomplished? By the same methods used by John the Baptist: preaching the gospel of repentance and baptism for the remission of sins.

In both cases the work had to be done authoritatively. John the Baptist had divine authority. He was sent of God, and the angel Gabriel made the announcement of his coming. Where did John obtain the gospel he taught? The scriptures do not explain. It is certain that the Jews were apostate at the time; hence he did not obtain from them the divine principles that he preached. Obviously it was through revelation that he was taught how to function.

So too with the Prophet Joseph Smith. The world was apostate when he came on the scene. He was confused by their so-called Christian teachings, and so he prayed for enlightenment. Which church was right among the contending denominations? The answer he was given was: none of them.

At the beginning of his work, Joseph had neither the knowledge to preach the correct doctrines nor the authority to do so. There had to be a restoration. He must obtain both the knowledge and the authority, or he could not perform his work. Joseph received both knowledge and authority, and thus he became, in the Lord's own words, "my messenger" to "prepare the way before me."

As John had to convert a group of believers who would accept the Christ when He appeared, so did Joseph Smith. And as John needed the proper knowledge and authority for his work, so did Joseph Smith. A restoration of the gospel took place. Angels came and gave Joseph divine authority. The Lord personally gave revelations by which Joseph was trained for his ministry.

John's work led to the establishment of the Church of Jesus Christ in his day. Joseph's work resulted in the same establishment in our day.

Only after Joseph Smith was clothed with divine authority, and only when he had been taught the divine truths through modern revelation, could he lay any foundation whatever for the Savior's coming.

In John's day, the preparation required only a limited effort, for the Savior did not leave the boundaries of little Palestine. Not so with Joseph and the Second Coming. The Lord has decreed that this advent will be seen worldwide. It will be so spectacular that the heavens will roll back, and all people will see his coming, the hosts of heaven with him. The stars will fall from their places, the sun will be eclipsed by the brightness of the Lord's appearance, and the moon will turn red.

The Savior will come in judgment with rewards for the righteous and destruction for the wicked. When he begins his millennial reign, there must be a cleansed earth to receive him. He will not reign over a sinful world. Hence wickedness will be overthrown, wars will end, and peace will come.

For such a vast and world-shaking appearance, a worldwide preparation is required. The people—those who will survive the great events of that day—will have to be taught, as the people in the Meridian of Time were taught by John the Baptist. A modern people must be prepared to receive the Lord.

This preparation will come only through a worldwide preaching of the restored gospel "in the hour of God's judgment." The scriptures say it would be brought to earth by angelic ministry (see Revelation 14:6-7) and then be preached in all the world as a warning to all nations (Matthew 24:14).

This preaching will convert the righteous who earnestly look forward to Christ's coming, and they will join his Church. It is to be by the same means used by John the Baptist.

To carry on the work in an orderly manner, the Lord fully restored his Church and priesthood in our day, and decreed that missionaries should go to every nation, kindred, tongue, and people, just as in ancient times.

All of this was done under the immediate direction of the Savior himself, who sent holy angels to minister to the Prophet Joseph Smith.

Joseph was the Lord's forerunner to begin the preparation for the Second Coming of the Lord. This work still goes on under the direction of living prophets who have succeeded Joseph, and it will continue worldwide until the Lord says "enough." Then he will come.

Millions of people now converted to the restored gospel are preparing to meet him. When the time comes, they will be ready.

Chapter 7

JOSEPH THE TEMPLE BUILDER

The Lord, whom ye seek shall suddenly come to his temple." (Malachi 3:1.)

So spoke Malachi as he foretold the glorious Second Coming of the Savior. Immediately there arises the question: What temple? The scripture says *his* temple. But does he have a temple on earth? Or will he?

Many structures in the world, both of ancient and modern origin, are called temples. The mighty buildings now being unearthed by archeologists in Mexico and Central and South America are called temples. Can it be to one of those that he will come? They are not *his* temples. They were temples of peoples who the archeologists claim offered human sacrifices. The true God was unknown to them. They were idolators.

Temples in India, China, and elsewhere in Asia have been erected to Buddha and other gods whom those nations revere. Will Christ come to any of them? Will he make His appearance in the beautiful shrine of Iemitsu at Nikko, Japan? Will it be to the "Temple of Heaven" complex at Peking, erected by the Ming dynasty?

Will it be to the Greek Doric temple at Segasta, Sicily, or to the temple of Ramses II at Abusimbe, Egypt? The Parthenon at Athens was a place of worship. So was the Roman temple of Fortuna Virilis, built by the Romans in the first century B.C. Will it be to either of these temples? Will it be to the mosque now standing on the site of Solomon's temple in Jerusalem?

To which temple will the Lord come in the day of judgment?

The temple referred to by Malachi obviously is related to the preparation provided by "the Lord's messenger," who, he says, "shall prepare the way before me." Then must this messenger be a temple builder? Must the temple be a modern temple rather than any of the ancient ones?

The whole work of this messenger is modern. It comes in the hour of God's judgment; Jesus will then judge the world. All will be strictly modern in every respect.

Joseph Smith was that prophetic messenger. Was he a temple builder? In revelations given by the Lord, he was instructed to build at least four temples—in Kirtland, Ohio; Far West, Missouri; Independence, Missouri; and Nauvoo, Illinois.

Due to the severe persecutions at the hands of their neighbors, the Saints were able to complete only two of those structures, in Kirtland and in Nauvoo. Sacred ordinances were performed in both.

These holy places form only a beginning to the temple-building program of the people raised up by the Lord through the instrumentality of the Prophet Joseph Smith. More than forty temples are now in operation, under construction, or approved for construction. And the work will go on.

Temple building is an integral part of the work of this last dispensation. The Church has been given three main divisions of activity: (1) the spreading of the gospel, (2) the perfecting of the Saints, teaching them to live Christlike lives, and (3) temple work.

These temples are not for ordinance work alone. Each one is literally the House of the Lord. Each one bears that insignia. Each is dedicated to him, so that now he has a place "to lay his head." (See Matthew 8:20; Luke 9:58.)

When the Lord spoke to Enoch about that day, he said that not only will the New Jerusalem be established in Jackson County, not only will he establish his tabernacle—his temple—there, but also Enoch and his city, which was taken into heaven anciently, will return as part of the restoration of the latter days. Note Enoch's record:

"And the Lord said unto Enoch: As I live, even so will I come in the last days, in the days of wickedness and vengeance, to fulfil the oath which I have made unto you concerning the children of Noah;

"And the day shall come that the earth shall rest, but before that day the heavens shall be darkened, and a veil of darkness shall cover the earth; and the heavens shall shake, and also the earth; and great tribulations shall be among the children of men, but my people will I preserve;

"And righteousness will I send down out of heaven; and truth will I send forth out of the earth, to bear testimony of mine Only Begotten; his resurrection from the dead; yea, and also the resurrection of all men; and righteousness and truth will I cause to sweep the earth as with a flood, to gather out mine elect from the four quarters of the earth, unto a place which I shall prepare, an Holy City, that my people may gird up their loins, and be looking forth for the time of my coming; for there shall be my tabernacle, and it shall be called Zion, a New Jerusalem.

"And the Lord said unto Enoch: Then shalt thou and all thy city meet them there, and we will receive them into our bosom, and they shall see us; and we will fall upon their necks, and they shall fall upon our necks, and we will kiss each other;

"And there shall be mine abode, and it shall be Zion, which shall come forth out of all the creations which I have made; and for the space of a thousand years the earth shall rest.

"And it came to pass that Enoch saw the day of the coming of the Son of Man, in the last days, to dwell on the earth in righteousness for the space of a thousand years;

"But before that day he saw great tribulations among the wicked; and he also saw the sea, that it was troubled, and men's hearts failing them, looking forth with fear for the judgments of the Almighty God, which should come upon the wicked.

"And the Lord showed Enoch all things, even unto the end of the world; and he saw the day of the righteous, the hour of their redemption, and received a fulness of joy." (Moses 7: 60-67.)

Chapter 8

THE WILDERNESS TABERNACLE

Each temple or tabernacle of ancient Israel was literally a house of the Lord. God came to those structures and directed the ministrations that took place in them, even designating the priesthood to officiate there.

The tabernacle that the Israelites carried with them through their forty-year journey in Sinai was indeed a remarkable house of the Lord. It was furnished with such elegance and wealth that it foreshadowed the opulence of Solomon's temple, which succeeded it. The Israelites called this holy place the Tabernacle of the Congregation.

When Moses was preparing to erect the tabernacle, he called upon the people to make donations for its construction. He asked them for contributions of gold, silver, brass, fine linens, ram skins dyed red, the skins of badgers, acacia woods, oil, spices, perfumes, and precious stones. (Exodus 25:1-7.) Gifts came in such profusion that he then issued a proclamation slowing down the process.

The structure was 45 feet long and 15 feet wide, surrounded by a courtyard 150 feet by 75 feet, which was formed by curtains suspended from rods of silver and wood. The wooden rods used to sustain the tent were covered with gold and silver, and the rings that held the curtains were of solid gold or silver.

The tabernacle was built within a year. When it was finished, a cloud hovered over it, and the glory of the Lord filled the sanctuary, signifying its acceptance by the Lord. The cloud continued to rest upon the tabernacle through most of the journeying of the Twelve Tribes.

During the journey, the Ark of the Covenant was deposited in the tabernacle in the Holy of Holies, as was a container holding a morsel of manna for future generations to see. (See Exodus 16:33.) Each time the tribes moved to a new location, the entire structure was folded away; and when a new camp was made, it was set up once again.

The Lord recognized the tabernacle as a sacred place; in fact, as *his* place. His glory was there. He spoke to his servants there. His sacred ordinances were performed there. In it he spoke face to face with Moses. Note just a few passages on this point:

"And Moses took the tabernacle, and pitched it without the camp, afar off from the camp, and called it the Tabernacle of the congregation. And it came to pass, that every one which sought the Lord went out unto the tabernacle of the congregation, which was without the camp.

"And it came to pass, when Moses went out unto the tabernacle, that all the people rose up, and stood every man at his tent door, and looked after Moses, until he was gone into the tabernacle.

"And it came to pass, as Moses entered into the tabernacle, the cloudy pillar descended, and stood at the door of the tabernacle, and the Lord talked with Moses.

"And all the people saw the cloudy pillar stand at the tabernacle door: and all the people rose up and worshipped, every man in his tent door.

"And the Lord spake unto Moses face to face, as a man speaketh unto his friend. And he turned again into the camp: but his servant Joshua, the son of Nun, a young man, departed not out of the tabernacle." (Exodus 33:7-11.)

In this tabernacle Moses was told that he would not be allowed to lead the people into Palestine:

"And the Lord said unto Moses, Behold, thy days approach that thou must die: call Joshua, and present yourselves in the tabernacle of the congregation, that I may give him a charge. And Moses and Joshua went, and presented themselves in the tabernacle of the congregation.

"And the Lord appeared in the tabernacle in a pillar of a

cloud: and the pillar of the cloud stood over the door of the tabernacle.

"And the Lord said unto Moses, Behold, thou shalt sleep with thy fathers; and this people will rise up, and go a whoring after the gods of the strangers of the land, whither they go to be among them, and will forsake me, and break my covenant which I have made with them." (Deuteronomy 31:14-16.)

The tabernacle was still in use in the days of King David:

"And they brought in the ark of the Lord, and set it in his place, in the midst of the tabernacle that David had pitched for it: and David offered burnt offerings and peace offerings before the Lord. And as soon as David had made an end of offering burnt offerings and peace offerings, he blessed the people in the name of the Lord of hosts." (2 Samuel 6:17-18.)

When David became king, the Ark of the Covenant was removed to the City of David; and when the Temple of Solomon was finished, the tabernacle was lost sight of.

As the Salt Lake Temple was nearing completion, J. M. Sjodahl, an assistant historian of the Church, wrote a pamphlet in which he said the following about ancient temples:

"It is a remarkable fact, as will appear in the following sketch, that the history of the temples reflects the condition of the people of God itself. Sanctuaries erected under the supervision of the Almighty are more than specimens of architecture. They are types of the Church on earth.

"The tabernacle of the wilderness, with the glorious presence of the Shekinah, was a symbol of the pilgrim church, guarded by day and by night by the angel of Jehovah; the gorgeous temple of Solomon was a reflex of the people at that time; the inferior building of Zerubbabel reflected the condition of the Jews returned from captivity, and the temple of Herod, with its splendid exterior but without the most sacred implements of worship, was an equally true symbol of the deplorable religious condition of the Jews at that time.

"We may draw the analogy further, and notice that the absence of any temple after the fall of Jerusalem indicates the absence from the earth of the true Church, while the rearing of temples in this age again proves that God has a people on earth.

"For the lesson of history is that when the temple fell the people of God were scattered, and when it again rose from its ruins the people gathered." *(Temples, Ancient and Modern* [Deseret News Co.], p. 2.)

Whether tents or solid structures, when God has commanded his people to erect temples for sacred purposes, each one in its turn has become a house or abiding place of the Lord. Whenever the Almighty has had a people on earth whom he has recognized as his own, he has commanded them to build such structures to his name. And the work goes on apace in our day.

On the outside walls of all of our modern temples appears the designation:

"HOLINESS TO THE LORD."

This same designation appeared anciently. (See Exodus 28:36; 39:30; Zechariah 14:20.)

Temples are houses of God in the most real sense, for there his authorized servants minister; there his sacred ordinances are performed, without which there is no exaltation in his holy presence. And there, if he so desires, he may find a place to rest his head.

Chapter 9

SUBSEQUENT TEMPLES

Solomon's temple, of course, is the most notable, the most costly, the most revered of all temples. Hosts of men were employed in its construction. The richest woods and the finest jewels and metals were used. The scriptures indicate that 30,000 men labored to provide the timber alone. For this timber, Solomon paid Hyrum, king of Tyre, in whose lands the trees were located, a yearly tribute of 20,000 measures of wheat and 20 measures of pure oil.

Some 60,000 stone cutters were employed, and 70,000 men were used as laborers to carry burdens from one place to another.

The general design of the temple was similar to that of the Tabernacle of the Congregation, though the entire structure was much more elaborately decorated. A large font was built within the temple, while the ark containing the tablets of stone listing the Ten Commandments was kept in the most holy place.

Because of the wickedness of the people both during and following the reign of Solomon, the temple was not used for long. The original splendor of the edifice lasted only thirty-four years, and at the death of Solomon an invading army desecrated it.

When Nebuchadnezzar invaded Palestine, he robbed the temple of its costly contents and set fire to the building as he carried the Jews off to Babylon.

The temple was reconstructed when Cyrus the Great permitted the Jews to return to their own homeland in 536 B.C. The foundation for the new structure was laid in 535 B.C., and the building was completed and dedicated in 516 B.C.

Although it was built on the same plan used by Solomon,

this new temple was plain in every respect because of the poverty of the people. During subsequent wars, the building again suffered from the depredations of enemies, especially in the time of the Maccabees.

The temple was "purified" and rededicated to the Lord in 163 B.C., but the people generally had become apostate by this time, with the rise of at least a half dozen dissenting factions of Judaism.

When Herod the Great came to power, he deposed the last of the Maccabean family and slew all of the Sanhedrin but two. Sixteen years before the birth of Christ, Herod authorized the repair and enlargement of the temple, seeking to win the favor of the Jews. It was said that for nine years, 18,000 men worked on the project. The work continued for about forty-six years altogether, but the building was destroyed in A.D. 70 when the Roman General Titus invaded Jerusalem. Thus the temples of the Lord in Palestine came to an end.

Numerous temples were also built in ancient America. Archeologists have uncovered only a few, which were obviously pagan structures erected to worship idols and to offer human sacrifices.

The Nephites built various temples. The first Nephi erected one similar to Solomon's temple, although not so grand. He wrote:

"I did teach my people to build buildings, and to work in all manner of wood, and of iron, and of copper, and of brass, and of steel, and of gold, and of silver, and of precious ores, which were in great abundance.

"And I, Nephi, did build a temple; and I did construct it after the manner of the temple of Solomon save it were not built of so many precious things; for they were not to be found upon the land, wherefore, it could not be built like unto Solomon's temple. But the manner of the construction was like unto the temple of Solomon; and the workmanship thereof was exceedingly fine." (2 Nephi 5:15-16.)

Jacob taught in the temple: "Wherefore I, Jacob, gave unto [the Nephites] these words as I taught them in the temple, having first obtained mine errand from the Lord." (Jacob 1:17.)

After the death of his brother Nephi, Jacob spoke to the people: "Wherefore, I must tell you the truth according to the plainness of the word of God. For behold, as I inquired of the Lord, thus came the word unto me, saying: Jacob, get thou up into the temple on the morrow, and declare the word which I shall give thee unto this people." (Jacob 1:17; 2:11.)

Mosiah summoned the people to the temple to hear King Benjamin: "And now, it came to pass that Mosiah went and did as his father had commanded him, and proclaimed unto all the people who were in the land of Zarahemla that thereby they might gather themselves together, to go up to the temple to hear the words which his father should speak unto them." (Mosiah 1:18.)

There was a temple also in the region governed by the wicked King Noah (Mosiah 11:12), apparently having been built by the faithful Zeniff, who organized that colony.

When the Savior appeared to the ancient Americans, the people met him near the temple in the land Bountiful: "And now it came to pass that there were a great multitude gathered together, of the people of Nephi, round about the temple which was in the land Bountiful; and they were marveling and wondering one with another, and were showing one to another the great and marvelous change which had taken place. And they were also conversing about this Jesus Christ, of whom the sign had been given concerning his death." (3 Nephi 11:1-2.)

We do not know what ordinances were performed in those structures, although we might assume that since Nephi built a temple after the manner of Solomon's, similar ordinances may have been performed there.

Throughout the ages, the people of God have had their temples, the most sacred of all their buildings. Therefore, it is not surprising that in the latter days the Lord "shall suddenly come to his temple," as Malachi predicted. But it will be to *his* temple, not to some worldly structure having no divine significance.

Chapter 10

THE PREDICTED JUDGMENT

Jesus himself talked about his coming when he appeared to the Prophet Joseph Smith at a conference of the Church at Fayette, New York, in January 1831. As he began his revelation, he fully identified himself:

"I am the same which spake, and the world was made, and all things came by me. I am the same which have taken the Zion of Enoch into mine own bosom; and verily, I say, even as many as have believed in my name, for I am Christ, and in mine own name, by the virtue of the blood which I have spilt, have I pleaded before the Father for them." (D&C 38:3-4.)

The Savior's description of his coming to Palestine has been given through modern revelation:

"It shall come to pass that he that feareth me shall be looking forth for the great day of the Lord to come, even for the signs of the coming of the Son of Man. And they shall see signs and wonders, for they shall be shown forth in the heavens above, and in the earth beneath. And they shall behold blood, and fire, and vapors of smoke.

"And before the day of the Lord shall come, the sun shall be darkened, and the moon be turned into blood, and the stars fall from heaven. And the remnant shall be gathered unto this place; and then they shall look for me, and, behold, I will come; and they shall see me in the clouds of heaven, clothed with power and great glory; with all the holy angels; and he that watches not for me shall be cut off. But before the arm of the Lord shall fall, an angel shall sound his trump, and the saints that have slept shall come forth to meet me in the cloud.

"Wherefore, if ye have slept in peace blessed are you; for as you now behold me and know that I am, even so shall ye come unto me and your souls shall live, and your redemption shall be perfected; and the saints shall come forth from the four quarters of the earth.

"Then shall the arm of the Lord fall upon the nations. And then shall the Lord set his foot upon this mount, and it shall cleave in twain, and the earth shall tremble, and reel to and fro, and the heavens also shall shake.

"And the Lord shall utter his voice, and all the ends of the earth shall hear it; and the nations of the earth shall mourn, and they that have laughed shall see their folly. And calamity shall cover the mocker, and the scorner shall be consumed; and they that have watched for iniquity shall be hewn down and cast into the fire.

"And then shall the Jews look upon me and say: What are these wounds in thine hands and in thy feet?

"Then shall they know that I am the Lord; for I will say unto them: These wounds are the wounds with which I was wounded in the house of my friends. I am he who was lifted up. I am Jesus that was crucified. I am the Son of God.

"And then shall they weep because of their iniquities; then shall they lament because they persecuted their king." (D&C 45:39-53.)

When he spoke of the New Jerusalem in America, he said:

"And it shall be called the New Jerusalem, a land of peace, a city of refuge, a place of safety for the saints of the Most High God; and the glory of the Lord shall be there, and the terror of the Lord also shall be there, insomuch that the wicked will not come unto it, and it shall be called Zion.

"And it shall come to pass among the wicked, that every man that will not take his sword against his neighbor must needs flee unto Zion for safety. And there shall be gathered unto it out of every nation under heaven; and it shall be the only people that shall not be at war one with another.

"And it shall be said among the wicked: Let us not go up to battle against Zion, for the inhabitants of Zion are terrible; wherefore we cannot stand. And it shall come to pass that the righteous shall be gathered out from among all nations, and shall come to Zion, singing with songs of everlasting joy." (D&C 45:66-71.)

He further explained: "Until that hour there will be foolish virgins among the wise; and at that hour cometh an entire separation of the righteous and the wicked; and in that day will I send mine angels to pluck out the wicked and cast them into unquenchable fire." (D&C 63:54.)

In the revelation designated by the Prophet Joseph Smith as "the olive leaf," the Lord talked about signs of his coming:

"After your testimony cometh wrath and indignation upon the people. For after your testimony cometh the testimony of earthquakes, that shall cause groanings in the midst of her, and men shall fall upon the ground and shall not be able to stand.

"And also cometh the testimony of the voice of thunderings, and the voice of lightnings, and the voice of tempests, and the voice of the waves of the sea heaving themselves beyond their bounds. And all things shall be in commotion; and surely, men's hearts shall fail them; for fear shall come upon all people.

"And angels shall fly through the midst of heaven, crying with a loud voice, sounding the trump of God, saying: Prepare ye, prepare ye, O inhabitants of the earth; for the judgment of our God is come. Behold, and lo, the Bridegroom cometh; go ye out to meet him.

"And immediately there shall appear a great sign in heaven, and all people shall see it together.

"And another angel shall sound his trump, saying: That great church, the mother of abominations, that made all nations drink of the wine of the wrath of her fornication, that persecuteth the saints of God, that shed their blood—she who sitteth upon many waters, and upon the islands of the sea—behold, she is the tares of the earth; she is bound in bundles; her bands are made strong, no man can loose them; therefore, she is ready to be burned. And he shall sound his trump both long and loud, and all nations shall hear it.

"And there shall be silence in heaven for the space of half an hour; and immediately after shall the curtain of heaven be unfolded, as a scroll is unfolded after it is rolled up, and the face of the Lord shall be unveiled; and the saints that are upon the earth, who are alive, shall be quickened and be caught up to meet him.

"And they who have slept in their graves shall come forth, for their graves shall be opened; and they also shall be caught up to meet him in the midst of the pillar of heaven—

"They are Christ's, the first fruits, they who shall descend with him first, and they who are on the earth and in their graves, who are first caught up to meet him; and all this by the voice of the sounding of the trump of the angel of God." (D&C 88: 88-98.)

Although Malachi says that the day of judgment will consume the wicked, he promises peace to the righteous:

"For, behold, the day cometh, that shall burn as an oven; and all the proud, yea, and all that do wickedly, shall be stubble: and the day that cometh shall burn them up, saith the Lord of hosts, that it shall leave them neither root nor branch.

"But unto you that fear my name shall the Sun of righteousness arise with healing in his wings; and ye shall go forth, and grow up as calves of the stall.

"And ye shall tread down the wicked; for they shall be ashes under the soles of your feet in the day that I shall do this, saith the Lord of hosts." (Malachi 4:1-3.)

Of the righteous, Malachi declared: "And they shall be mine, saith the Lord of hosts, in that day when I make up my jewels; and I will spare them, as a man spareth his own son that serveth him. Then shall ye return, and discern between the righteous and the wicked, between him that serveth God and him that serveth him not." (Malachi 3:17-18.)

The prophet Nephi spoke of these tribulations, saying:

"For the time soon cometh that the fulness of the wrath of God shall be poured out upon all the children of men; for he will not suffer that the wicked shall destroy the righteous.

"Wherefore, he will preserve the righteous by his power, even if it so be that the fulness of his wrath must come, and the righteous be preserved, even unto the destruction of their enemies by fire. Wherefore, the righteous need not fear; for thus saith the prophet, they shall be saved, even if it so be as by fire.

"Behold, my brethren, I say unto you, that these things must shortly come; yea, even blood, and fire, and vapor of smoke must come; and it must needs be upon the face of this earth; and it cometh unto men according to the flesh if it so be that they will harden their hearts against the Holy One of Israel.

"For behold, the righteous shall not perish; for the time surely must come that all they who fight against Zion shall be cut off. . . ."

"And the righteous need not fear, for they are those who shall not be confounded. But it is the kingdom of the devil, which shall be built up among the children of men, which kingdom is established among them which are in the flesh. . . .

"And the time cometh speedily that the righteous must be led up as calves of the stall, and the Holy One of Israel must reign in dominion, and might, and power, and great glory.

"And he gathereth his children from the four quarters of the earth; and he numbereth his sheep, and they know him; and there shall be one fold and one shepherd; and he shall feed his sheep, and in him they shall find pasture.

"And because of the righteousness of his people, Satan has no power; wherefore, he cannot be loosed for the space of many years; for he hath no power over the hearts of the people, for they dwell in righteousness, and the Holy One of Israel reigneth." (1 Nephi 22:16-19, 22, 24-26.)

Chapter 11

THE PREPARATION

The scriptures tell us that three messengers would precede the Lord's coming. Malachi speaks of a mortal messenger who "shall prepare the way before me." (Malachi 3:1.) That messenger, as we have seen, is the Prophet Joseph Smith, the temple builder. A vital part of his work was temple building. Without such preparation, without a divinely directed temple-building activity, the world would not be ready to receive their Lord. Without it, how could he come to his temple, his very own?

The faithful Saints will build many temples, but there will be one great structure in the New Jerusalem where the Lord will make his appearance. Is it not altogether fitting that he should come to a sacred and hallowed sanctuary erected especially to his own name? And there he will come! The Saints who build it "shall be mine, saith the Lord of hosts, in that day when I make up my jewels; and I will spare them, as a man spareth his own son that serveth him." (Malachi 3:17.)

The second messenger assigned to a latter-day work is mentioned not by Malachi, but by John the Revelator. This angel's destined flight through the midst of heaven was to restore the gospel of Christ, which long had been lost to mankind. The good word was then to be preached to all nations, warning mankind of the approaching visitation by the Savior. (See Revelation 14:6-7; Matthew 24:14.) John said that this angel's time was to be in the hour of God's judgment, a modern event.

Moroni was the other angel. He brought the pure gospel contained in the Book of Mormon.

The third messenger was Elijah the prophet, who was assigned to come in the latter days, before the great and dreadful day of the Lord. (Malachi 4:5-6.) What of his coming? What did Malachi say about it? What gives Elijah importance in connection with the Second Coming of the Savior? He lived hundreds of years before Jesus was born in the flesh. What possible relationship could he have to the latter days?

Elijah was taken into heaven without tasting death, riding to the skies in a glorious chariot. He came back in the days of Jesus' mortality, as a companion to the prophet Moses. The two prophets appeared to the Savior and his disciples on the Mount of Transfiguration.

Elisha, who succeeded Elijah, is not given such prominence. Not even Isaiah, Jeremiah, Samuel, or Ezekiel are mentioned in connection with the Lord's Second Coming. Is Elijah some very unusual person whose mission is not revealed in the Bible, but whose work we should study and know? Who is Elijah? Who was he while on earth, and what is his destined latter-day work?

Chapter 12

ELIJAH THE PROPHET

The sins of King Solomon led to the destruction of his kingdom. Then other wicked kings took possession and led the people into further apostasy. Idolatry, tolerated by Solomon, now was encouraged by the rulers who followed him.

In the midst of this corruption, Elijah the prophet appeared. He is spoken of as Elijah the Tishbite, "who was of the inhabitants of Gilead." (1 Kings 17:1.) Since he was known as a "Tishbite," he may have been born in Tishbeh, a village of Galilee.

Unheralded previously in scripture, Elijah appeared suddenly in the court of the wicked King Ahab and his Phoenician wife Jezebel. Some scholars call the period of Ahab's reign Israel's worst.

Jezebel was largely to blame for conditions existing at the time. A pagan, she was determined to make idolatry—the worship of Baal—the religion of the entire nation. She stopped at nothing—not murder, nor intrigue, nor even the miracles of Elijah. Her influence carried from Israel, the kingdom of Ahab, over into Judah, where her daughter Athaliah had married the son of Jehoshaphat. Jezebel was considered the greatest religious fanatic of her time.

It was in the midst of this state of things that the Lord sent Elijah to Ahab, to denounce the king for his grievous transgressions and to expose Jezebel and hers. Elijah stood before this wicked pair and announced: "As the Lord God of Israel liveth, before whom I stand, there shall not be dew nor rain these years, but according to my word." (1 Kings 17:1.)

Thus began a three-year drouth in the land. Crops and streams dried up, and the people suffered starvation. Still Ahab and Jezebel refused to yield.

Elijah himself was cared for miraculously by the Lord. He stayed near the brook Cherith "that is before Jordan," and there he was fed by ravens, which brought him bread and meat every day. He drank from the brook until it no longer flowed. The Lord then sent him to Zidon, where a widow and her only son lived. For her kindness in taking Elijah into her home and feeding him from what she thought was her last meager supply of food, the Lord caused that her cruse of oil never ran dry and her barrel of meal never emptied.

While Elijah lived there, the widow's son died, and she became bitter. She cried out at Elijah, "What have I to do with thee, O thou man of God? art thou come unto me to call my sin to remembrance, and to slay my son?" By the ministry of Elijah, the boy's life was restored. Elijah then returned to the court of Ahab, who demanded: "Art thou he that troubleth Israel?" Elijah replied, "I have not troubled Israel; but thou, and thy father's house, in that ye have forsaken the commandments of the Lord, and thou hast followed Baalim."

Elijah asked Ahab to gather the people together, including all of the priests of Baal. There were many of them, 450 in one area and 400 more "among the groves" who ate at Jezebel's table.

Elijah addressed the gathering: "How long halt ye between two opinions? if the Lord be God, follow him: but if Baal, then follow him. And the people answered him not a word."

Elijah, determined to wipe out idolatry, demanded a showdown before all the people to demonstrate which they should serve, the God of Israel or Baal, the Phoenician idol. He called for two bullocks, one for himself and one for the priests of Baal. He planned that each bullock should be put on an altar as a sacrifice, one to Baal and the other to the Lord.

Elijah then challenged the 450 priests of Baal who were assembled there to call down fire from heaven to consume their bullock. They failed. Elijah mocked them for their failure. The priests cut themselves with knives to further beseech their god, but to no avail. They cried, they shouted, and they prayed until evening, but still no response.

Then came Elijah's turn. He was certain the Lord would reply to him. To impress the people even more, he poured large quantities of water upon his sacrifice, soaking even the surroundings of the altar.

"And it came to pass at the time of the offering of the evening sacrifice, that Elijah the prophet came near, and said, Lord God of Abraham, Isaac, and of Israel, let it be known this day that thou art God in Israel, and that I am thy servant, and that I have done all these things at thy word. Hear me, O Lord, hear me, that this people may know that thou art the Lord God, and that thou hast turned their heart back again.

"Then the fire of the Lord fell, and consumed the burnt sacrifice, and the wood, and the stones, and the dust, and licked up the water that was in the trench. And when all the people saw it, they fell on their faces: and they said, The Lord, he is the God; the Lord, he is the God.

"And Elijah said unto them, Take the prophets of Baal; let not one of them escape. And they took them: and Elijah brought them down to the brook Kishon, and slew them there."

Then Elijah called for rain, and it came. The drouth was broken.

Jezebel, furious with Elijah, said to him, "So let the gods do to me, and more also, if I make not thy life as the life of one of them by to morrow about this time." Elijah left the area, and angels ministered to him. (1 Kings 17-19.)

Chapter 13

ELIJAH TRANSLATED

Elijah came on the scene about 890 years before Christ. He was not any ordinary prophet; he had powers far beyond most of the prophets of Old Testament times. Bearing power to seal the heavens so that they would not give any rain, he also had power to bring the moisture back again. Holding authority to strike the river Jordan, he halted the water and he and Elisha walked across dry shod.

By modern revelation we discover that Elijah was chosen of the Lord for a special work, not only in mortality but also following his death. He came back to earth twice as an angel of God, once to the Savior in the Transfiguration and the second time to Joseph Smith in fulfillment of Malachi's remarkable prophecy.

Elijah was also given special powers related to the fulness of the gospel, both in the days of Peter and Paul and in our own time. Truly he was one of the greatest of the prophets.

Elijah did not die according to the usual pattern of men. He was translated—taken into heaven without tasting death—and rode on high in a fiery chariot drawn by heavenly horses. That event deserves mention.

The Lord one day spoke to Elijah and said: "Go, return on thy way to the wilderness of Damascus: and when thou comest, anoint Hazael to be king over Syria: and Jehu the son of Nimshi shalt thou anoint to be king over Israel: and Elisha the son of Shaphat of Abel-meholah, shalt thou anoint to be prophet in thy room. . . .

"So he departed thence, and found Elisha the son of Shaphat, who was plowing with twelve yoke of oxen before him, and he with the twelfth: and Elijah passed by him, and cast his mantle upon him. And he left the oxen, and ran after Elijah, and said, Let me, I pray thee, kiss my father and my mother, and then I will follow thee. And he said unto him, Go back again: for what have I done to thee? And he returned back from him, and took a yoke of oxen, and slew them, and boiled their flesh with the instruments of the oxen, and gave unto the people, and they did eat. Then he arose, and went after Elijah, and ministered unto him." (1 Kings 19:15-16, 19-21.)

But Elijah was not yet finished with Ahab and Jezebel.

"The word of the Lord came to Elijah the Tishbite, saying, Arise, go down to meet Ahab king of Israel, which is in Samaria: behold, he is in the vineyard of Naboth, whither he is gone down to possess it. And thou shalt speak unto him, saying, Thus saith the Lord, Hast thou killed, and also taken possession? And thou shalt speak unto him, saying, Thus saith the Lord, In the place where dogs licked the blood of Naboth shall dogs lick thy blood, even thine.

"And Ahab said to Elijah, Hast thou found me, O mine enemy? And he answered, I have found thee: because thou hast sold thyself to work evil in the sight of the Lord. Behold, I will bring evil upon thee, and will take away thy posterity, and will cut off from Ahab him that pisseth against the wall, and him that is shut up and left in Israel, and will make thine house like the house of Jeroboam the son of Nebat, and like the house of Baasha the son of Ahijah, for the provocation wherewith thou hast provoked me to anger, and made Israel to sin.

"And of Jezebel also spake the Lord, saying, The dogs shall eat Jezebel by the wall of Jezreel." (1 Kings 21:17-23.)

Both the king and his evil wife died as the prophet had said.

Elijah seems to have been told in advance that he would be taken into heaven without tasting death. We read:

"It came to pass, when the Lord would take up Elijah into heaven by a whirlwind, that Elijah went with Elisha from Gilgal. And Elijah said unto Elisha, Tarry here, I pray thee; for the Lord hath sent me to Beth-el. And Elisha said unto him, As the Lord liveth, and as thy soul liveth, I will not leave thee. So they went down to Beth-el.

"And the sons of the prophets that were at Beth-el came

forth to Elisha, and said unto him, Knowest thou that the Lord will take away thy master from thy head to day? And he said, Yea, I know it; hold ye your peace. And Elijah said unto him, Elisha, tarry here, I pray thee; for the Lord hath sent me to Jericho. And he said, As the Lord liveth, and as thy soul liveth, I will not leave thee. So they came to Jericho.

"And the sons of the prophets that were at Jericho came to Elisha, and said unto him, Knowest thou that the Lord will take away thy master from thy head to day? And he answered, Yea, I know it; hold ye your peace. And Elijah said unto him, Tarry, I pray thee, here; for the Lord hath sent me to Jordan. And he said, As the Lord liveth, and as thy soul liveth, I will not leave thee. And they two went on.

"And fifty men of the sons of the prophets went, and stood to view afar off: and they two stood by Jordan. And Elijah took his mantle, and wrapped it together, and smote the waters, and they were divided hither and thither, so that they two went over on dry ground.

"And it came to pass, when they were gone over, that Elijah said unto Elisha, Ask what I shall do for thee, before I be taken away from thee. And Elisha said, I pray thee, let a double portion of thy spirit be upon me. And he said, Thou hast asked a hard thing: nevertheless, if thou see me when I am taken from thee, it shall be so unto thee; but if not, it shall not be so.

"And it came to pass, as they still went on, and talked, that, behold, there appeared a chariot of fire, and horses of fire, and parted them both asunder; and Elijah went up by a whirlwind into heaven.

"And Elisha saw it, and he cried, My father, my father, the chariot of Israel, and the horsemen thereof. And he saw him no more: and he took hold of his own clothes, and rent them in two pieces. He took up also the mantle of Elijah that fell from him, and went back, and stood by the bank of Jordan; and he took the mantle of Elijah that fell from him, and smote the waters, and said, Where is the Lord God of Elijah? and when he also had smitten the waters, they parted hither and thither: and Elisha went over.

"And when the sons of the prophets which were to view at Jericho saw him, they said, The spirit of Elijah doth rest on Elisha. And they came to meet him, and bowed themselves to the ground before him." (2 Kings 2:1-15.)

Chapter 14

ELIJAH'S MISSION

The prophet Malachi referred to a latter-day mission of the prophet Elijah, who was to return before the great and dreadful day of the Lord to turn the hearts of the fathers to the children and the hearts of the children to their fathers.

This prophecy has confused Bible scholars throughout the years. Why should Elijah come in the latter days? What could he do to turn the hearts of the generations toward each other?

Many question the visit of Elijah and Moses to Peter, James, and John at the Transfiguration of the Savior. That, too, has puzzled readers of the Bible.

Both Moses and Elijah were translated and did not die the usual death known to mortals. As heavenly messengers, they both appeared on the Mount of Transfiguration in New Testament times.

President Joseph Fielding Smith explains:

"There was a reason for the translation of Elijah. Men are not preserved in that manner unless there is a reason for it. Moses was likewise taken up—though the scriptures say that the Lord buried him upon the mountain.

"Of course the writer of that wrote according to his understanding; but Moses, like Elijah, was taken up without tasting death, because he had a mission to perform. . . .

"When Moses and Elijah came to the Savior and to Peter, James and John upon the Mount, what was their coming for? Was it just some spiritual manifestation to strengthen these three apostles? Or did they come merely to give comfort unto the Son of God in his ministry and to prepare him for his crucifixion? No! That was not the purpose.

"I will read it to you. The Prophet Joseph Smith has explained it in the *Church History*, volume 3, page 387, as follows:

"'The Priesthood is everlasting. The Savior, Moses, and Elias [Elijah, in other words], gave the keys to Peter, James, and John, on the mount, when they were transfigured before him. The Priesthood is everlasting—without beginning of days or end of years; without father, mother, etc. If there is no change of ordinances, there is no change of Priesthood. Wherever the ordinances of the Gospel are administered, there is the Priesthood.'. . .

"From that we understand why Elijah and Moses were preserved from death—because they had a mission to perform, and it had to be performed before the crucifixion of the Son of God, and therefore it could not be done in the spirit. They had to have tangible bodies.

"Christ is the first fruits of the resurrection; therefore if any former prophet had a work to perform preparatory to the mission of the Son of God, or to the dispensation of the Meridian of Time, it was essential that they be preserved to fulfil that mission in the flesh. For that reason Moses disappeared from among the people and was taken up into the mountain, and the people thought he was buried by the Lord; the Lord preserved him, so that he could come at the proper time and restore his keys, on the heads of Peter, James and John, who stood at the head of the dispensation of the Meridian of Time. He reserved Elijah from death that he might also come and bestow his keys upon the heads of Peter, James and John and prepare them for their ministry.

"But, one says, the Lord could have waited until after his resurrection and then they could have done it. It is quite evident, due to the fact that it did so occur, that it had to be done before; and there was a reason. There may have been other reasons, but that is one reason why Moses and Elijah did not suffer death in the flesh, as other men do.

"After the resurrection of Christ, of course they could easily have passed through death and the resurrection, and then as resurrected beings come to fulfil a mission of like import in the Dispensation of the Fulness of Times, and this is exactly what they did.

"Why was Elijah reserved? What keys did he hold? What keys did he bestow on Peter, James and John? Exactly the same keys that he bestowed upon the head of Joseph Smith and Oliver Cowdery. And what were they? Some of you may be saying the keys of baptism for the dead. No, it was not that. Some of you may be thinking it was the keys of the salvation of the dead. No, it was not that. That was only a portion of it.

"The keys that Elijah held were the keys of the everlasting priesthood, the keys of the sealing power, which the Lord gave unto him. And that is what he came and bestowed upon the head of Peter, James and John, and that is what he gave to the Prophet Joseph Smith; and that included a ministry of sealing for the living as well as the dead—and it is not confined to the living and it is not confined to the dead, but includes them both. . . .

"You know when the Lord took Moses out of the midst of the children of Israel, he took the higher priesthood also, and he left the Aaronic Priesthood and the Levitical Priesthood, and added unto that the law of Moses. But down through the ages from the days of Moses, whenever the Lord had a special mission for a prophet, that prophet held the Melchizedek Priesthood. But it was not conferred upon many—it was confined to certain of the prophets, whose mission required it. Joseph Smith the prophet said:

"'Elijah was the last Prophet that held the keys of the Priesthood, and who will, before the last dispensation, restore the authority and deliver the keys of the Priesthood, in order that all the ordinances may be attended to in righteousness. It is true that the Savior had authority and power to bestow this blessing; but the sons of Levi were too prejudiced. "And I will send Elijah the Prophet before the great and dreadful day of the Lord," etc., etc. Why send Elijah? Because he holds the keys of the authority to administer in all the ordinances of the Priesthood; and without the authority is given, the ordinances could not be administered in righteousness.' (*History of the Church* 4:211.)" (Joseph Fielding Smith, *Elijah the Prophet and His Mission* [Deseret Book, 1957], pp. 22, 27-31.)

Chapter 15

THE SEALING KEYS

The keys held by Elijah the prophet were the keys of the sealing power of the priesthood. The Prophet Joseph Smith said:

"The spirit, power, and calling of Elijah is, that ye have power to hold the key of the revelation, ordinances, oracles, powers and endowments of the fullness of the Melchisedeck Priesthood and of the kingdom of God on the earth; and to receive, obtain, and perform all the ordinances belonging to the kingdom of God, even unto the turning of the hearts of the fathers unto the children, and the hearts of the children unto the fathers, even those who are in heaven.

"Malachi says, 'I will send you Elijah the prophet before the coming of the great and dreadful day of the Lord: and he shall turn the heart of the fathers to the children, and the heart of the children to their fathers, lest I come and smite the earth with a curse.'. . .

"In the days of Noah, God destroyed the world by a flood, and He has promised to destroy it by fire in the last days; but before it should take place, Elijah should first come and turn the hearts of the fathers to the children, etc.

"Now comes the point. What is this office and work of Elijah? It is one of the greatest and most important subjects that God has revealed. He should send Elijah to seal the children to the fathers, and the fathers to the children. . . .

"I wish you to understand this subject, for it is important; and if you will receive it, this is the spirit of Elijah, that we redeem our dead, and connect ourselves with our fathers which are in heaven, and seal up our dead to come forth in the first resurrection; and here we want the power of Elijah to seal those who dwell on earth to those who dwell in heaven. This is the power of Elijah and the keys of the kingdom of Jehovah.

"Let us suppose a case. Suppose the great God who dwells in heaven should reveal Himself to Father Cutler here, by the opening heavens, and tell him, 'I offer up a decree that whatsoever you seal on earth with your decree, I will seal it in heaven; you have the power then; can it be taken off? No. Then what you seal on earth, by the keys of Elijah, is sealed in heaven; and this is the power of Elijah, and this is the difference between the spirit and power of Elias and Elijah. . . .

"Again: the doctrine or sealing power of Elijah is as follows:—If you have power to seal on earth and in heaven, then we should be wise. The first thing you do, go and seal on earth your sons and daughters unto yourself, and yourself unto your fathers in eternal glory. . . . I will walk through the gate of heaven and claim what I seal, and those that follow me and my counsel." *(History of the Church* 6:251-53.)

President Joseph Fielding Smith has commented on these passages as follows:

"The power and the authority held by Elijah then, lies in the sealing ordinances, and more particularly those pertaining to the Holy Temple. Only one man at a time holds the keys of this sealing power on the earth.

"According to the revelation 'all covenants, contracts, bonds, obligations, oaths, vows, performances, connections, associations, or expectations,' that pertain to the exaltation must be entered into and made with the sanction and approval of the sealing authority of the one who holds the keys of Priesthood in the Church. This one is always the President of the Church, who is President of the High Priesthood.

"He may, and does, delegate the sealing authority to others so that they may officiate in the Temples in all the ordinances which pertain to the exaltation in the celestial kingdom; but no man can take this honor unto himself.

"The President may at any time he is so disposed revoke the privilege and bring an end to the authority of any individual who may be called and set apart to perform these sacred ordinances. Any man who presumes to have authority to perform these sealing ordinances which belong to the House of the Lord when it has not been given him by the one who holds the keys of authority, is an imposter and a fraud. It is a most astonishing thing that in view of what the Lord has revealed there are those who rise up from time to time claiming that they have authority and no one can take it from them.

"There is order in the Church. While the majority of the male members hold the Priesthood and are called to officiate in a general way in the ordinances of the Gospel, yet, we, one and all, should realize that it is the power vested in the President of the Church by virtue of the keys he holds which come from Elijah in particular and from other prophets of old in general, which makes valid the authority which we possess. Without that central authority with its commanding keys and the privilege extended to the men holding the Priesthood by this one person who presides, the acts of those who are ordained to the Priesthood 'could not be administered in righteousness.'

"Peter, James and John restored the Melchizedek Priesthood, out of which all the offices come; but the ordinances of the Gospel which are performed by virtue of that High Priesthood receive their final sanction and approval by virtue of the keys of authority. In other words they are bound in heaven as well as on earth by virtue of the sealing power.

"The question naturally arises in the inquiring mind, 'Why would the whole earth be smitten with a curse had not Elijah come with the keys of sealing which he held?' This is explained in the discourses on this subject by the Prophet Joseph Smith.

"The family organization must be intact. First husbands and wives must be sealed for time and for all eternity. When this is done children born to them belong to them for time and all eternity, and the family units are preserved.

"Parents who have been married out of the new and everlasting covenant must be sealed for time and all eternity and then have their children sealed to them. When this is done the ordinance is just as valid as it is in the case of those who were originally married according to the law of the Lord. In like manner the children who are living may have the same ordinances performed for their ancestors who are dead. Then each generation must be joined to the one which went on before.

"In this way eventually all the families which are entitled to celestial exaltation are joined together from generation to generation back to the time of our first parents, Adam and Eve. This will not all be done before the coming of our Lord, but the great work of the Millennium will be the temple ordinances for the dead who are worthy to receive it.

"The sealing power of Elijah makes it possible for this joining of the families, generation to generation, back to the beginning. Now, if these keys of authority were not here, then the work of sealing, by which the family units are preserved, could not be performed; then the binding power by which all blessings are sealed in heaven as well as on earth would be lacking.

"If this were so the earth would be smitten with a curse, for all work which had been done without these binding or sealing ordinances, would fall to the ground unfulfilled.

"But now we have the fulness of the power of the Priesthood. The Lord has restored the keys and authorities of all the dispensations and has made it possible by the power of Elijah to make every act performed by authority of force when men are dead or out of the world.

"Let us remember that all contracts, bonds, oaths, or performances, which are not entered into by the authority of this sealing power, are of no efficacy or virtue after men are dead. The house of the Lord is a house of order and everything in it is obedient to divine law.

"When a man assumes authority which he does not have and becomes a law unto himself, according to the word of the Lord he is not justified and must remain filthy still.

"Let each member of the Church reflect carefully upon these things and see to it that he or she is in perfect harmony with that which the Lord has revealed, and that all ordinances are received under the hands of those who are officially called and endowed with power from on high." *(The Utah Genealogical and Historical Magazine* 27:50-53.)

Chapter 16

TO REDEEM THE DEAD

Toward the end of his mortal ministry, the Prophet Joseph Smith discoursed freely on the subject of Elijah's mission and salvation for the dead. He clearly stated that the mission of that ancient prophet was directly associated with temple work, genealogical research, and the salvation of us all, living and dead.

He spoke as follows:

"What you seal on earth, by the keys of Elijah, is sealed in heaven; and this is the power of Elijah, and this is the difference between the spirit and power of Elias and Elijah; for while the spirit of Elias is a forerunner, the power of Elijah is sufficient to make our calling and election sure; and the same doctrine, where we are exhorted to go on to perfection, not laying again the foundation of repentance from dead works, and of laying on of hands, resurrection of the dead, etc.

"We cannot be perfect without the fathers, etc. We must have revelation from them, and we can see that the doctrine of revelation far transcends the doctrine of no revelation; for one truth revealed from heaven is worth all the sectarian notions in existence.

"This spirit of Elijah was manifest in the days of the apostles, in delivering certain ones to the buffetings of Satan, that they might be saved in the day of the Lord Jesus. They were sealed by the spirit of Elijah unto the damnation of hell until the day of the Lord, or revelation of Jesus Christ.

"Here is the doctrine of election that the world has quarreled so much about; but they do not know anything about it.

"The doctrine that the Presbyterians and Methodists have quarreled so much about—once in grace, always in grace, or falling away from grace, I will say a word about. They are both wrong. Truth takes a road between them both, for while the Presbyterian says 'once in grace, you cannot fall;' the Methodist says: 'You can have grace today, fall from it to-morrow, next day have grace again; and so follow on, changing continually.' But the doctrine of the Scriptures and the spirit of Elijah would show them both false, and take a road between them both; for, according to the Scripture, if men have received the good word of God, and tasted of the powers of the world to come, if they shall fall away, it is impossible to renew them again, seeing they have crucified the Son of God afresh, and put Him to an open shame; so there is a possibility of falling away; you could not be renewed again, and the power of Elijah cannot seal against this sin, for this is a reserve made in the seals and power of the Priesthood.

"I will make every doctrine plain that I present, and it shall stand upon a firm basis, and I am at the defiance of the world, for I will take shelter under the broad cover of the wings of the work in which I am engaged. It matters not to me if all hell boils over; I regard it only as I would the crackling of the thorns under a pot.

"A murderer, for instance, one that sheds innocent blood, cannot have forgiveness. David sought repentance at the hand of God carefully with tears, for the murder of Uriah; but he could only get it through hell: he got a promise that his soul should not be left in hell.

"Although David was a king, he never did obtain the spirit and power of Elijah and the fullness of the Priesthood; and the Priesthood that he received, and the throne and kingdom of David is to be taken from him and given to another by the name of David in the last days, raised up out of his lineage.

"Peter referred to the same subject on the day of Pentecost, but the multitude did not get the endowment that Peter had; but several days after, the people asked 'What shall we do?' Peter says, 'I would ye had done it ignorantly,' speaking of crucifying the Lord, etc. He did not say to them, 'Repent and be baptized, for the remission of sins;' but he said, 'Repent ye therefore, and be converted, that your sins may be blotted out, when the times of refreshing shall come from the presence of the Lord.' (Acts 3:19.)

"This is the case with murderers. They could not be baptized for the remission of sins for they had shed innocent blood. . . .

"The spirit of Elias is first, Elijah second, and Messiah last. Elias is a forerunner to prepare the way, and the spirit and power of Elijah is to come after, holding the keys of power, building the Temple to the capstone, placing the seals of the Melchisedec Priesthood upon the house of Israel, and making all things ready; then Messiah comes to His Temple, which is last of all." (*History of the Church* 6:252-54.)

Chapter 17

ELIJAH'S VISITATION

The modern appearance of the Prophet Elijah occurred at the completion of the temple in Kirtland, Ohio. The Saints had labored long and hard to erect that building and dedicate it to the Lord. The dedication was held on March 27, 1836, at a solemn assembly in the temple. The building was filled to capacity long before the service began.

As on the ancient day of Pentecost, the heavens were opened, visions were seen, and, at the close of the dedicatory prayer, which had been given by revelation, the Saints shouted "Hosanna, hosanna, hosanna, to God and the Lamb." They then sealed the exercises with their united "Amen, Amen, and Amen." (Joseph Fielding Smith, *Essentials in Church History* [Deseret Book, 1974], p. 159.)

On Sunday, April 3, 1836, a meeting was held in the temple, and the sacrament was administered. Following this great event, Joseph Smith and Oliver Cowdery retired to a space near the pulpit, secluded by veils that were dropped while they engaged in prayer.

President Joseph Fielding Smith wrote concerning their experience as follows:

"The Savior appeared to them standing on the breastwork of the pulpit and blessed them, accepting the building in his name. After this vision closed, the heavens were again opened, and Moses appeared committing to them the keys of the gathering of Israel; Elias, who lived in the days of Abraham, then appeared, and committed to them the keys of the dispensation of the Gospel of Abraham. Then another glorious vision burst upon them and Elijah appeared and committed to them the keys, in fulfilment of the prediction of Malachi, of the turning of the hearts of the fathers to the children, and the hearts of the children to the fathers, which was to be done before the coming of the great and dreadful day of the Lord." (Ibid., pp. 160-61.)

The coming of Elijah is recorded in the Doctrine and Covenants:

"After this vision had closed, another great and glorious vision burst upon us; for Elijah the prophet, who was taken to heaven without tasting death, stood before us, and said:

"Behold, the time has fully come, which was spoken of by the mouth of Malachi—testifying that he [Elijah] should be sent, before the great and dreadful day of the Lord come—to turn the hearts of the fathers to the children, and the children to the fathers, lest the whole earth be smitten with a curse—therefore, the keys of this dispensation are committed into your hands; and by this ye may know that the great and dreadful day of the Lord is near, even at the doors." (D&C 110:13-16.)

Thus was fulfilled the prophecy made by Malachi the prophet, centuries before Christ, with special reference to the last days. If Elijah had not come, if the keys of his priesthood powers had not been restored, if the hearts of fathers and children had not been turned to each other, the earth would have been smitten with a curse. But he came, the keys were restored, and the work of turning of the hearts of the generations was begun. The curse was stayed.

Note that Elijah came "before the great and dreadful day of the Lord." This dates his coming to modern times. The other angel of the restoration, which is spoken of by John the Revelator, flying "in the midst of heaven, having the gospel" to be restored, also came in modern times. His appearance also was dated: "The hour of [God's] judgment." (Revelation 14:6-7.) That messenger was Moroni.

The entire restoration event was modern. All ancient things were done away, and the gospel was on earth anew; the Church of Jesus Christ was brought back anew and now the work goes forward in preparation for the Lord, who will suddenly come to his temple.

Chapter 18

RESEARCH FOLLOWS

It is remarkable how, after being dormant over the centuries, genealogical research activity began so quickly following the coming of Elijah. People who had never heard of Elijah became interested—almost overwhelmingly—in searching out their dead, members and nonmembers of the Church alike.

In nearly every nation in the world, fascination with genealogical research has grown. Hundreds of societies formed for the express purpose of finding and preparing human pedigrees have been organized in recent years. Hundreds of thousands of individuals are engaged in searches for the records of their ancestors. Patriotic and hereditary societies in which eligibility for membership is based upon proof of descent from some honored statesman, soldier, or pioneer have been organized by the score.

Many genealogical magazines are being published in various nations, and some newspapers of wide circulation run genealogical columns. Large libraries devoted exclusively to genealogical material and family history have been established in various nations. Hundreds of thousands of volumes of such data have been published within the last century, and so great has been the demand for this kind of printed matter that public libraries in most cities of the United States have found it necessary to establish genealogical departments, in many cases under the direction of trained genealogists.

Through microfilm, additional records in many countries are being copied and preserved. These microfilm records are now among the richest sources of genealogical information.

The appearance of numerous books of fiction with a genealogical or family history theme is another indication of the reaction of people to this subject. Some of these books have even been best sellers.

In England, France, Germany, Sweden, Denmark, Norway, Scotland, and other European countries, governments have required the preservation of genealogical data and in many cases have set up archives for this purpose.

Since Elijah, whose coming created this interest, was destined by prophecy to appear in the latter days, "before the great and dreadful day of the Lord," it remains to determine if this vast genealogical activity is of modern origin.

The *Encyclopedia Americana* says: "In the United States, genealogy was generally neglected until the latter part of the 19th century, when the organization of patriotic, State and colonial societies . . . aroused an interest in genealogy."

The *New Standard Encyclopedia* states: "There has been a growing interest, especially in the United States, in matters pertaining to genealogical research, and it forms a very important part of history. This is largely due to the growth of patriotic and hereditary societies which have flourished in the United States since 1890."

These two authorities set the latter part of the nineteenth century as the period when general interest in the subject appeared.

The formation of patriotic and hereditary societies stimulated genealogical pursuits. *Nelson's Encyclopedia* describes such societies thus: "In the United States, organizations in which the members bound together for patriotic work, and in many cases eligibility is dependent upon descent from an ancestor who participated in the event which the society commemorates. These societies, especially the hereditary ones, publish registers with the pedigree of their members and the records of their ancestors. They celebrate anniversaries of important events in history and foster fraternal feeling among the survivors of wars and their descendants."

Lists of these societies and their aims, particularly concerning ancestral studies, may be found in any large encyclopedia. The organizations include such groups as the Sons of the American Revolution, the Daughters of the American Revolution, the Society of Mayflower Descendants, and the Order of Descendants of Colonial Governors.

Their work reveals that the "hearts of the children" are being turned to their fathers in more ways than the preparation of family histories and pedigrees. Interest is shown in the preservation of historical buildings, erection of monuments on sites where their forefathers won glory, the marking of graves, and the construction of memorial parks.

Many of these societies were formed about the year 1890, but some came into being as early as 1850. Since it takes a few years for the interest of individuals to crystallize into the organization of societies with a special interest in ancestry, we must look to a year slightly earlier than 1850 to arrive at a time when such interest began.

In response to a letter asking the date when genealogical interest began in America, F. A. Virkus, executive director of the Institute of American Genealogy, wrote: "In 1844 the New England Historical Genealogical Society was formed in Boston, and genealogy in America really dates with the founding of this society."

To show how little was the interest in this subject in 1844, Josephine E. Rayne, librarian of the New England Historical Genealogical Society, wrote: "When our society was formed, a single bookcase was sufficient to hold the entire library, and had the society then possessed one copy of each American publication devoted wholly to genealogy, a single shelf would have been ample for that division of its library. However, we now have in our specialized library some 80,000 volumes and several thousand pamphlets."

By way of still further arriving at the precise time when widespread genealogical interest began in America, we have a most interesting paragraph from the register of the New England Society for 1847, in which the founders discuss the reasons for the formation of their organization in 1844: "The period has arrived when an awakening and growing interest is felt in this country in the pursuit, and especially the result of historical and genealogical research and when the practical importance, both to individuals and to society, of the knowledge obtained from such investigations begins to be appreciated. The existence and activities of the historical, antiquarian and statistical societies which have arisen within a few years past in most of the other states of the Union is sufficient evidence of the fact."

We have shown that international interest was aroused in genealogy beginning a few years before 1844. According to the scripture, Elijah was to originate that interest. Then Elijah must have come a few years before 1844 in order to have started (according to prophecy) a movement that burst into activity at that time.

And so he did!

A passage in the first epistle of Peter refers to the flood of Noah's day, saying that "a few, that is eight souls, were saved by water." Exactly "a few, that is eight" years before 1844, the date when the first genealogical society was organized, Elijah made his appearance in fulfillment of the words of Malachi. He came in 1836.

Is there any evidence that Elijah appeared?

Every genealogical society, library, and magazine; every genealogical record; every name on every page of every pedigree; every individual in the United States and foreign nations engaged in seeking after his dead—every one of these is a witness that Elijah came, because each indicates the fulfillment of that prophet's mission "to turn the hearts of the children to their fathers," as foretold by Malachi.

The results of Elijah's mission are all about us. The evidence is conclusive. There is no room for doubt: Elijah has come! One of the greatest of the prophecies has been fulfilled. It is one of the most convincing of the signs of all times, testifying that the great and dreadful day of the Lord is near.

Not only does this vast genealogical interest testify to the truth of Elijah's coming; it also gives testimony to the divine calling of men to whom he appeared in modern times. It declares in indisputable truth that the men to whom Elijah appeared in that temple in Kirtland were chosen of the Almighty, and that the work they instituted with the assistance of Elijah was heaven-inspired.

Through the revelations of God, and empowered by angelic ministry, they organized The Church of Jesus Christ of Latter-day Saints and gave to the world, in its purity, the gospel of Christ. They received ordination to the priesthood from John the Baptist and Peter, James, and John, and with that power they preached anew the gospel in its restored simplicity.

The Prophet Joseph Smith explained the purpose of Elijah's coming and the reason behind his "turning the hearts of the children to their fathers." He taught that genealogical work has a definite place in the plan of salvation, a direct relationship to the fundamentals of the Christian religion.

So we have a great twofold activity in the earth as a result of Elijah's modern mission. One is the worldwide activity in the preparation of family histories and pedigrees, providing the necessary identification for those who have lived on the earth and are now dead. The other is the intense activity of members of The Church of Jesus Christ of Latter-day Saints in building temples and performing in them the sacred ordinances of the gospel that all who come unto Christ may be saved in his kingdom.

This temple work could not be done without the identification provided through worldwide genealogical research. The two activities go hand in hand to accomplish the work of the Lord as it was instituted through the Prophet Joseph Smith and is now carried on by his people.

This is why the Mormons build temples.

Chapter 19

SALVATION FOR LIVING AND DEAD

The Lord's plan of salvation is applicable to all peoples and all circumstances. It reaches the dead and the living, the rich and the poor.

Through the ages, prophets were sent to teach the principles of the gospel to all who would hear. Their messages were essentially the same, although each had his own particular niche in the over-all program of God.

So it was with Elijah. His mission related to both the ancients and us of today. It related to the living and the dead. His was a distinctive calling, and he was specially endowed for it. Since he was to turn the hearts of the fathers (the dead) to the children (the living), and the hearts of the living to the dead, his mission related to both sides of the veil, the here and the hereafter.

The vast majority of earth's populations are now dead. The living are but a tiny minority among all the inhabitants of this planet. To tie both fathers and children—the various generations—together in common interest was something that could be achieved only by divine assistance. Elijah was ordained for just such a task.

Justification for this simultaneous turning of the hearts of both fathers and children, living and dead, is found abundantly in the justice of God. He is no respecter of persons. One who is dead is as dear to him as one who is living, for all live unto him. (See Luke 20:38.) Everyone belongs to His family, both those who have died on this earth, and those who still live here. And there are millions of unborn spirits yet to come. All are his children.

God desires that each of us may become perfect, even as he

is. (Matthew 5:48.) Hence, his efforts are not confined to the narrow existence we know as mortality. Indeed, he is active on both sides of the veil.

The Savior had this in mind in the early part of his earthly ministry. In his conversation with Nicodemus, the Lord strongly stressed the importance of baptism, and he made no exceptions, either for living or dead. He told Nicodemus that he could not even see the kingdom of heaven without this ordinance. Then could anyone else?

Did Jesus not also say that God so loved the world that he gave his only begotten Son that whosoever believeth in him should not perish, but have everlasting life?

And did he not say that God sent not his Son into the world to condemn it, but that through him all could be saved if they would obey him? "He that believeth on Him is not condemned," he said; only those who refuse to believe are condemned. (John 3:4-21.)

How do people come to believe? By hearing his word. There is no other way. For this reason he sent his apostles into the world to teach and baptize believers. (Mark 16:15-17.) He desired that everyone should hear and obey. "Have I any pleasure at all that the wicked should die? saith the Lord God: and not that he should return from his ways, and live?" (Ezekiel 18:23.)

But how could the vast majority of God's children—the dead—hear the gospel equally with the small minority living on earth? Obviously he would be fair to both groups, not being a respecter of persons.

The living and the dead must hear the glad word; otherwise they would not be treated equally and could not choose whether to serve him or not, either in life or in death. Serve him in death? How could that be?

The spirits of the departed never die. They are always alive and alert, and continue relationships one with another. Only the physical body dies. For this reason the Savior, out of consideration for all who had not heard his teachings, said: "Verily, verily, I say unto you, He that heareth my word, and believeth on him that sent me, hath everlasting life, and shall not come into condemnation; but is passed from death unto life."

Thus he revealed his fairness to everyone. Then he continued: "Verily, verily, I say unto you, The hour is coming, and now is, when the dead shall hear the voice of the Son of God: and they that hear shall live."

But even that was not enough. He continued: "Marvel not at this: for the hour is coming, in the which all that are in the graves shall hear his voice, and shall come forth; they that have done good, unto the resurrection of life; and they that have done evil, unto the resurrection of damnation." (John 5:24-25, 28-29.)

What a view of the infinite justice and mercy of God!

How did this instruction to the dead come about? How did they actually hear his voice? Or did they?

Of course they heard him—most emphatically yes!

While the Lord's body lay in the tomb following his crucifixion, his immortal and eternal spirit visited the equally immortal and eternal spirits of human beings who had passed away previously. Those who died in the flood of Noah's day are mentioned specifically. And so we read:

"For Christ also hath once suffered for sins, the just for the unjust, that he might bring us to God, being put to death in the flesh, but quickened by the Spirit: by which also he went and preached unto the spirits in prison; which sometime were disobedient, when once the longsuffering of God waited in the days of Noah, while the ark was a preparing, wherein few, that is, eight souls were saved by water." (1 Peter 3:18-20.)

How divine, how kind and merciful his plan! All will have equal opportunity for salvation, whether living or dead.

Peter explains the divine purpose still further: "For for this cause was the gospel preached also to them that are dead, that they might be judged according to men in the flesh, but live according to God in the spirit." (1 Peter 4:6.)

Then those who were dead had full opportunity to hear the

message, and if they chose to do so, they could repent and "live according to God in the spirit."

It is interesting to note the rendering given this verse by translators of other faiths:

"Because he is their judge too, the dead had to be told the Good News as well, so that though, in their life on earth, they had been through the judgment that comes to all humanity, they might come to God's life in the spirit." (Jerusalem Bible.)

"For this is why the gospel was preached even to the dead, that though judged in the flesh like men, they might live in the spirit like God." (Catholic version, British Revised Standard Translation.)

"Why was the Gospel preached to those who are dead? In order that, although in the body they suffered the sentence common to men, they might in the spirit be alive with the life of God." (New English Bible.)

"For that is why the dead also had the Gospel preached to them—that it might judge the lives they lived as men and give them also the opportunity to share the eternal life of God in the spirit." (Phillips Version.)

"For this purpose the Good News was declared also to the dead, they they might be judged as to the flesh from the standpoint of men, but might live as to the spirit from the standpoint of God." (New World New Testament.)

Can anyone doubt that the dead heard the gospel in their own realm? Can we deny that the Savior himself brought it to them? Then did not the dead have opportunity to so adjust their status that they could "live according to God in the spirit"?

Christ's preaching to the dead opened the way for a fulfillment of Malachi's words regarding Elijah. When these imprisoned souls heard the truths of salvation in the spirit world, they understood the requirements of the gospel and that baptism was one of them. In their condition they could not receive baptism, for it was an ordinance to be performed only in mortality. Their bodies were in the grave, long since returned to dust. But vicarious baptism performed by mortals in behalf of the dead would suffice. God gave it as the only way of applying the cleansing blood of Christ to their souls.

No doubt the dead were given such an explanation during the preaching of the gospel. Then would not their hearts turn back toward mortality? And in whom would they be most interested? Certainly not strangers. It would be their own living descendants.

So the hearts of the dead fathers turned to their living descendants in the hope of obtaining vicarious baptisms through their efforts. And thus Elijah's mission began.

The Lord's plan of salvation in this way spanned both the here and the hereafter. What a blessing to mankind! What a fulfillment of one part of Malachi's prediction that Elijah's power would turn the hearts of past generations to the later ones!

Chapter 20

WHAT OF BAPTISM?

The Savior was completely clear in declaring the necessity of baptism as part of his gospel. Righteous as Nicodemus may have been, he could not even see the kingdom without baptism, and he was no exception.

Jesus taught and practiced baptism. His disciples performed this ordinance under his direction. They baptized even more than did John the Baptist. (John 4:1-2.) Christ's message to the world, through his disciples who were sent out among all nations, declared: "He that believeth and is baptized shall be saved." (Mark 16:16.)

His disciples carried out this decree in their own ministry. Note the words of Peter: "Repent, and be baptized every one of you in the name of Jesus Christ for the remission of sins, and ye shall receive the gift of the Holy Ghost." (Acts 2:38.)

Note the words of Paul: "For as many of you as have been baptized into Christ have put on Christ." (Galatians 3:27.)

And the words of Ananias to the newly converted Paul: "And now why tarriest thou? arise, and be baptized, and wash away thy sins, calling on the name of the Lord." (Acts 22:16.)

And when Cornelius was converted, what did Peter say? "Can any man forbid water, that these should not be baptized, which have received the Holy Ghost as well as we? And he commanded them to be baptized in the name of the Lord. Then prayed they him to tarry certain days." (Acts 10:47-48.)

Baptism was the means of entering Christ's Church: "For as many of you as have been baptized into Christ have put on Christ." (Galatians 3:27.)

Baptism saves us, according to Peter, who spoke of Noah's escape from the flood, "The like figure whereunto even baptism doth also now save us." (1 Peter 3:21.)

Baptism is required of all who can believe and repent, even the dead, for admission into the kingdom of God.

Peter's epistle teaches that the dead were taught the gospel in order that they might "live according to God in the spirit." (1 Peter 4:6.) Could they live according to God while still in their sins? If not, how could they be freed of their guilt? By what means are we granted forgiveness, or remission of sins, as the scripture speaks of it? Peter gave the answer in very plain terms: "Repent, and be baptized every one of you in the name of Jesus Christ for the remission of sins." (Acts 2:38.) This is the answer.

When Ananias took care of the newly converted Paul, he said, "Arise, and be baptized, and wash away thy sins." (Acts 22:16.)

When John the Revelator wrote to the seven churches in Asia, he referred to Jesus Christ, who "loved us, and washed us from our sins in his own blood." (Revelation 1:5.)

And how is that blood applied to our sins? In baptism, because the purpose of that ordinance is precisely to wash away our sins, to grant us remission, to cleanse us, and to make us fit for Christ's kingdom.

How can this be applied to the dead?

The departed whom Christ visited while his body lay in the tomb were very wicked when they lived in the days of Noah. Yet they were given the gospel teachings after death, the purpose being to help them live according to God in the spirit world.

Could they completely obey the laws of God without baptism? No one else could. Were those wicked ones of Noah's day now to be given some special privilege and allowed to "live according to God in the spirit" without the one and only gospel ordinance that could cleanse them of their sins? Since God is no respecter of persons, he most certainly would not give any special favors to the very ones he destroyed in the flood when they defied him and his prophet Noah, and who gloried in their sins. Baptism is essential for all because "all have sinned, and come short of the glory of God." (Romans 3:23.)

When Christ preached the gospel to the dead, did he teach the whole gospel or only part of it? Baptism is basic to the gospel. Would he have omitted it? "He that believeth and is baptized shall be saved," Mark wrote. (Mark 16:16.)

Then what about the dead? Could there be baptism for them? By vicarious ministrations, yes. And such baptisms became a part of the true Christian procedure.

This was proven by Paul when he wrote his great treatise on the resurrection. Part of his defense of the resurrection and the reality of an afterlife was the fact that baptisms were being performed for the dead. "Else what shall they do which are baptized for the dead, if the dead rise not at all? why are they then baptized for the dead?" (1 Corinthians 15:29.)

The living officiated for and in behalf of the dead. Here we have the answer.

Critics have assailed this as an unexplainable passage, but the doctrine is clear, and it is supported by modern translations of the Bible. Note, for example, the New English Bible: "Again, there are those who receive baptism on behalf of the dead. Why should they do this? If the dead are not raised to life at all, what do they mean by being baptized on their behalf?" And does this not thereby indicate that the dead do need baptism?

The Jerusalem Bible (Catholic), speaking of the fact of the resurrection, says: "If this were not true, what do people hope to gain by being baptized for the dead? If the dead are not ever going to be raised, why be baptized on their behalf?" This passage shows plainly that baptism does benefit people after death.

And the New American Version, published by the Catholic Church, declares under a caption "Practical Faith": "If the dead are not raised, what about those who have themselves baptized on behalf of the dead? If the raising of the dead is not a reality, why be baptized on their behalf?"

When Billy Graham published his version of the Bible, the passage appeared in this way: "If the dead will not come back to life again, then what point is there in people being baptized for those who are gone? Why do it unless you believe that the dead will some day rise again?"

So the blessings derived from baptism extend beyond death. All Bible translations agree, ancient and modern. Baptism was performed in the early Church for and in behalf of the dead who could not receive it otherwise. This historic truth, so plainly taught by the apostle Paul, was evidence of the resurrection, and Paul so used it.

But conversely, is not the status of our resurrection evidence that baptism is required for salvation in the hereafter, and that vicarious baptism was an accepted practice of the early Christians and the Lord?

Chapter 21

THE HEARTS DID TURN

We have seen how the hearts of the fathers of previous generations turned to their descendants still on earth. When they, being dead, learned the principles of the gospel, they understood the necessity of baptism, without which they could not enter the kingdom of heaven.

But how would baptism be provided? Baptism is an earthly ordinance to be performed in water, and hence it is related strictly to mortality. The bodies of the departed had long since moldered in the grave and could not be baptized by immersion in water.

Baptism would have to be performed on earth in behalf of the dead, vicariously by people still in mortality. Who could be expected to do such a work for them? Not a stranger. Who but their own relatives, their blood descendants?

So the hearts of the "fathers" in the realm of the dead have turned to their relatives on earth, hoping that they would be baptized on their behalf. Thus has the first part of Malachi's prophecy been fulfilled.

How can the living children learn about this doctrine? How can they know what is expected of them?

Interest of living people in their dead ancestors is a fact of long standing. Note the Chinese, for example, who are known almost above all other nations for venerating their ancestors. The ancient Greeks provided for their loved ones as they crossed the river Styx at death. The Egyptians embalmed their dead and furnished food and drink, boats, and even servants for them on their journey to the other world. Norsemen buried boats with their dead chieftains to insure an easy passage to Valhalla, there to enjoy the feasts awaiting them as guests of their greatest warrior, Odin of the North. The American Indians have long regarded the burial places of their forebears as sacred premises.

Modern peoples differ from the ancients in that they have discarded any interest in mythological traditions pertaining to the dead. Involved in their own affairs, they give scant thought to their ancestors. They do not believe in either the river Styx or Valhalla. A great many are not even sure that there is a life to come.

But to meet the needs of the departed dead for vicarious baptism, according to the Lord's plan, the living must be inspired to develop an interest in their forebears. It must not be like that of the ancients, for old mythologies had nothing to do with salvation in God's kingdom. A new and different concern is required.

To help their forefathers, genealogical study is required. Pedigrees must be compiled. Identification is needed to perform vicarious ordinances. This will turn the hearts of the children to their fathers in a meaningful way, but how is it to be accomplished? How may people today learn about the precious doctrine of salvation for the dead? It is not taught in their churches. Bible scholars have been highly skeptical of the meaning of 1 Corinthians 15:29, which refers to baptism for the dead. The very idea is scorned by modern preachers. Many prefer to burn candles for their dead.

How can modern children know what is expected of them? Left to themselves, they are helpless, but not so the Lord. He has intervened through the mission of Elijah!

The ministry of the prophet relates to both the living and the dead. The power bestowed upon him has generated a mighty upsurge in genealogical research.

Malachi's prediction foresaw this development. We have seen how the hearts of the dead have been turned to the living. Now the attention of the living is being directed toward their dead. So the second part of Malachi's prophecy is coming true.

After the coming of Elijah in 1836, genealogical research

began to take on greater interest, on a small scale at first, but then in ever-increasing measure. Almost spontaneously, people in many lands were possessed of a passion to learn about their ancestors. Governments began to require information on the ancestries of their citizens. Great amounts of money were spent on such efforts, not to mention the investments of private organizations and single families and individuals.

The records thus compiled have provided the information needed to identify the ancestors for whom vicarious baptisms are to be performed. Otherwise such ordinances are of no value.

So now the two interests spoken of by Malachi have come together. The fathers have had their hearts turned to their descendants on earth as the gospel preached in the spirit world has established their need for baptism.

The children in mortality have been inspired to perform genealogical research and vicarious ordinances for their dead kindred, with proper identification in each instance. Thus their hearts have been turned to their fathers.

The spirit of Elijah pervades both sides of the veil. A community of interest has been established between living and dead. The hearts have been turned. The work has begun.

Elijah's mission was so important that without it the earth would have been smitten with a curse. (Malachi 4:6.) But he came, and the children on earth have responded. Genealogies have been and are being compiled. Hundreds of millions of names are now available for the vicarious work being done in our temples.

Malachi was a true prophet. He spoke of our day. We are building the kingdom as he foresaw it, with temples in many places. The great and dreadful day of the Lord draws nigh. And who may abide the day of his coming? The Saints—they who seek first the kingdom of God and his righteousness—they will abide the day. They will be spared from the tribulations. They will meet him when he comes!

INDEX

Abraham paid tithes, 13
Ahab, 39-40, 43
Alma refers to Abraham, 13
Angels minister to Joseph Smith, 21
Apostasy: Malachi lived in day of, 3-5; Joseph Smith lived in day of, 20
Ark of the Covenant, 25, 27
Athaliah, 39

Baal, worship of, 39-41
Baptism: preached by forerunners, 19; necessity of, 68-71, 72
Book of Mormon: tells of last days, 1-2; sealed portion to be revealed, 15; is witness of accuracy of Bible, 18
Bountiful, temple in, 31

Church of Jesus Christ, 20, 23
Cloud over tabernacle, 25-27
Cowdery, Oliver, visions of, 56-57
Cyrus the Great, 4, 29

David puts Ark of Covenant in tabernacle, 27
Dead: salvation for, 63-67; baptism for, 69-71, 72-73
Doctrine and Covenants refers to Malachi, 5-6
Doctrine of election, 53-54
Drouth, 39-40

Education, the Lord believes in, 16
Election, doctrine of, 53-54
Elias: spirit of, 53; vision of, 56
Elijah: return of, predicted, 2-3, 17; spoke of Malachi, 6; was third messenger, 37-38; denounces Ahab, 39; confronts priests of Baal, 40-41; was chosen for special work, 42; anoints Elisha, 42-43; predicts death of Ahab and Jezebel, 43; is translated, 43-45; mission of, 46-48, 61-62; held keys of priesthood, 48; spirit of, 49-50, 53-55; power and authority of, 50-52; visitation of, 56-57
Elisha, 42-45
Enoch, 23-24
Ezra, 5

Families, sealing of, 51-52

Genealogical societies, 59-60
Genealogical research, 53, 58-62, 73-74
Grace, 53-54
Graham, Billy, 70-71
Gratitude, law on, 11-12

Hearts, turning of, 49-50, 57, 62, 67, 72-74
Herod the Great, 30
Holy of Holies, 25

Idolatry, 4, 39

Jacob taught in temple, 30-31
Jehoshaphat, 39
Jesus Christ: considered Malachi's prophecies vital, 1; used Malachi's words to teach tithing, 11; commands us to study scriptures, 15-16; gave Nephites words of Malachi, 16-17; spoke of Second Coming, 32-33; spoke of New Jerusalem, 33-34; appeared in Kirtland Temple, 56
Jezebel, 39-41, 43
John the Baptist was forerunner, 19
Judgment, day of, 32-36
Justice of God, 63-65

King James Version, 17-18
Knowledge of forerunner, 19-20

Maccabees, 30
Malachi: speaks to our generation, 1-3, 6; received revelations from the

Father, 2; foretold Joseph Smith and temple building, 2, 37; foretold Elijah's return, 2-3, 37-38; lived in day of apostasy, 3, 5; personal life of, is unknown, 4; joined Nehemiah and Ezra in rebuking Jews, 5; references to, in Book of Mormon and D&C, 5-6; warned against unworthy sacrifices, 7-8; decried marriages to heathen women, 8-9; preaches tithing, 11-2; warns of day of judgment, 35; true prophet, 74
Manna, 26
Marriage within own faith, 8-10
Messenger(s): Joseph Smith as, 2, 22-23, 37; three, 37-38
Millennium, 1
Mission of Elijah, 46-48
Moroni, 6, 37
Mosiah summoned people to temple, 31
Moses: on law of sacrifice, 7; on unlawful marriages, 10; taught tithing, 13; erected tabernacle, 25; spoke to Lord in tabernacle, 26-27; came back as companion to Elijah, 38; at Transfiguration, 46; reason for translation of, 47; appeared in Kirtland Temple, 56

Nebuchadnezzar, 29
Nehemiah, 4-5, 9
Nephi, 30, 35-36
New Jerusalem, 23-24, 33-34, 37
Noah, wicked king, 31

"Olive leaf" revelation, 34-35

Palestine, Jesus' coming to, 32-33
Plan of salvation, 63-67
Priests disregard divine laws, 8-10
Prophecies of latter days, 1-3, 6

Rayne, Josephine E., 60-61
Redemption of the dead, 53-55
Repentance preached by forerunners, 19
Revelation called "olive leaf," 34

Sacrifice, unworthy, 7-8, 11
Salvation, 53-55, 63-67
Scriptures, studying, 15-16
Sealing power, 48-52
Second Coming: Jesus quotes Malachi on, 17; Joseph Smith was forerunner of, 19-21; to be worldwide advent, 20-21
Sjodahl, J. M., 27-28
Smith, Joseph: is special messenger, 2, 37; taught tithing, 13-14; was unlearned man, 18; was forerunner of Second Coming, 19-21; was temple builder, 22-23, 37; explained missions of Moses and Elijah, 46, 48; on spirit of Elijah, 49-50; on salvation for dead, 53-55; visions of, in Kirtland Temple, 56-57
Smith, Joseph F., 6
Smith, Joseph Fielding: on translation of Moses and Elijah, 46-48; on sealing authority, 50-52; on visions in Kirtland Temple, 56-57
Solomon, 9; temple of, 27, 29
Spirit of Elijah, 49-50, 74

Tabernacle of the Congregation, 25-27, 29
Temple(s): Saints to build, 2; reconstruction of, in Jerusalem, 4, 29-30; many buildings called, 22; building of, in latter days, 23, 37, 62; tabernacle was similar to, 25-28; of Solomon, 27, 29-30; ancient, 27-28; God commands us to build, 28; destroyed by Titus, 30; built by Nephites, 30-31
Temple work, 23, 53
Ten Commandments, 11, 29
Tithing, 11-14
Titus, Roman general, 30
Transfiguration of Savior, 46
Translation of Elijah, 43-45, 46-48
Tribulations, Nephi speaks of, 35-36

Urim and Thummim, 18

Virkus, F. A., 60
Visions in Kirtland Temple, 56-57

Widow who cared for Elijah, 40

Zeniff, 31